Academic Writing for International Students of Business

Academic Writing for International Students of Business is the first book specially designed to assist overseas students studying Business or Economics courses in English. Most courses expect students to complete a variety of writing tasks as part of their assessment, such as essays, reports and projects. For many students these can be a major concern, but this book explains the writing process from start to finish and practises all the key writing skills.

Academic Writing for International Students of Business is clearly organised and can be used either with a teacher or for self-study. It is divided into four main parts:

- The writing process, from assessing sources to proof-reading the completed work
- Elements of writing, practising such skills as giving definitions and examples
- Accuracy in writing, with 15 units on areas from abbreviations to verb tenses
- Writing models, which illustrate emails, CVs, reports and longer essays.

This pattern makes it easy for teachers or students to find the help they need with writing tasks. All the units include extensive practice exercises, and a full answer key is included. All the material has been thoroughly tested and revised.

This is an up-to-date course that reflects the interests and issues of contemporary Business studies. Critical reading, avoiding plagiarism and working in groups are dealt with in detail. This practical and easy-to-use guide will help students planning to progress to a career with international companies or organisations, where proficiency in written English is an important asset.

Stephen Bailey is a freelance teacher and writer of materials for English for Academic Purposes. He has previously worked in the Czech Republic, Japan, Malaysia and Spain and has taught international students for many years at the University of Nottingham, UK.

Academic Writing for International Students of Business

Stephen Bailey

Routledge
Taylor & Francis Group

LONDON AND NEW YORK

First edition published 2011
by Routledge
2 Park Square, Milton Park, Abingdon, Oxon OX14 4RN

Simultaneously published in the USA and Canada
by Routledge
711 Third Avenue, New York, NY 10017

Routledge is an imprint of the Taylor & Francis Group, an informa business

Typeset in Galliard by
Florence Production Ltd, Stoodleigh, Devon
Printed and bound in Great Britain by
MPG Books Group, UK

British Library Cataloguing in Publication Data
A catalogue record for this book is available from the British Library

Library of Congress Cataloging-in-Publication Data
Bailey, Stephen, 1947–
 Academic writing for international studies of business/
 Stephen Bailey. – 1st ed.
  p. cm.
  Includes bibliographical references and index.
 1. Authorship. 2. Academic writing. 3. Business writing.
 I. Title.
 PN151.B26 2011
 808′.06665–dc22   2010014023

ISBN13: 978–0–415–56470–0 (hbk)
ISBN13: 978–0–415–56471–7 (pbk)
ISBN13: 978–0–203–84157–0 (ebk)

Contents

Acknowledgements

I would like to thank the many staff and students at the Centre for English Language Education (CELE) at the University of Nottingham who have helped pilot these materials. In particular I should mention Ann Smith, Steve Dewhirst, Sandra Haywood, John Rabone, Richard Lee and John Hall who have helped me unravel some of the finer points of academic language. Additional thanks are due to the lecturers at Nottingham University Business School, Nottingham Business School, Birmingham Business School and Manchester Business School who took the time to explain their various concerns regarding the written work of their international students.

My wife Rene has again provided me with invaluable support, encouragement and help with many aspects of academic writing during the development of this project. Final thanks are due to my daughter, Sophie, for helping me keep the whole subject in perspective!

Introduction for teachers

This course has been developed to help international students of Business and Economics with their writing assignments in English at both under-graduate and postgraduate level. There is significant research (e.g. Bacha and Bahous, 2008) to suggest that such students tend to underestimate the difficulty of completing these tasks, in terms of both the reading and writing skills involved.

In addition, lecturers at Nottingham University Business School, Nottingham Business School, Birmingham Business School and Manchester Business School have shared their concerns with me about the writing challenges faced by their international students. These focus on difficulties with vocabulary, and the lack of critical thinking skills, with regard to reading and writing. They are also concerned with students' failure to answer the specific question and their inability to develop answers logically. Issues around plagiarism and referencing skills are also significant worries.

Academic Writing for International Students of Business sets out to address these and other problems directly. Although the trend towards the internationalisation of business courses has substantial benefits, and inter-national students are not expected to write perfect English, it should be understood that accurate and effective language use is an essential skill for such students. What may be individually minor problems with prepositions, word endings, spelling and articles can result, in sum, in essays that are barely comprehensible to the best-motivated marker.

This book has been designed for use both in the classroom and for self-study/reference. This is a recognition that foundation, in-sessional and pre-sessional courses are inevitably time-constrained, and that some students may prefer or need to work by themselves. All exercises can be done individually or in pairs and groups. Students can check their work using the answer key. The book is designed for ease of access and simplicity of reference, which is achieved via the structure:

Part	Topic	Application
1	**The writing process** from reading to proof-reading	Classroom use
2	**Elements of writing** from argument to working in groups	Classroom use and self-study
3	**Accuracy in writing** from abbreviations to verb tenses	Classroom use, self-study and reference
4	**Writing models** from letters to longer essays	Self-study and reference
5	**Answers to exercises**	

The material in this course has been extensively tested in the classroom, but improvements can always be achieved in future editions. Therefore I would be very glad to receive any comments or suggestions about the book from teachers of Business, Economics or English for Academic Purposes.

Stephen Bailey
Email: education@routledge.com

Reference

Bacha, N. and Bahous, R. (2008). 'Contrasting Views of Business Students' Writing Needs in an EFL Environment'. *English for Specific Purposes* 27, 1, 74–93

Introduction for students

This book is designed to help you succeed in the writing tasks you may be given as part of your Business or Economics course. The kinds of writing that you are asked to do may be different from the assignments you have done before, and for some this may also be the first time you have had to write long essays in English.

Your teachers know that English is not your native language and will be sympathetic to the problems you have in your writing. But at the same time you will want to learn to write as clearly and accurately as possible, not only to succeed in your current course but also in preparation for your career. Almost all companies and organisations expect their staff to be able to communicate effectively in written English, as well as orally. Therefore, during your studies you have the ideal opportunity to learn to write well, and this book can help you achieve that goal.

In addition to accuracy, students on Business courses are expected to take a critical approach to their sources. This means that your teachers will expect you to question and evaluate everything you read, asking whether it is reliable or relevant. You are also expected to carefully refer to the sources of all your ideas using a standard system of referencing. *Academic Writing for International Students of Business* will help you to develop these skills.

Managing your time

Many teachers complain about work that is handed in late or shows signs of having been finished in a hurry. This leads to poor marks, and can be avoided by better time management. This means planning your time carefully from the start of the course so that your work is never late or rushed.

■ **Decide if the following ideas about time management are true or false:**

(a) Essay deadlines are often several months after the course starts.   (T/F)

(b) The best way to plan an assignment is to use some kind of wall chart.   (T/F)

(c) Reading and note-making often take longer than writing.   (T/F)

(d) The best time to study is after midnight.   (T/F)

(e) It's a good idea to make time every day to relax with friends.   (T/F)

In fact, all of these are true except for (d): it's better to study during the day and then get a good night's sleep. The key point is to schedule the work for each task week by week, so that you allocate time for drafting, rewriting and proof-reading. By doing this you will avoid the last-minute panic that leads to poor marks and having to re-take courses.

The book can be used either with a teacher or for self-study and reference. Each unit contains practice exercises, which can be checked using the answer key. For ease of use it is divided into the following sections:

Part 1 The writing process

This follows the process of writing from the reading stage through to proof-reading.

Part 2 Elements of writing

The key writing skills, organised alphabetically from Argument to Working in groups.

Part 3 Accuracy in writing

This section revises and practises areas of grammar and vocabulary, again arranged alphabetically, from Abbreviations to Verb tenses.

Part 4 Writing models

Gives examples of letters and emails, CVs, survey reports and longer essays.

Part 5 Answers to exercises

I would be very glad to receive comments and suggestions on any aspect of this book to help develop future editions.

Stephen Bailey
Email: education@routledge.com

Academic writing quiz

■ **How much do you know about academic writing? Find out by doing this fun quiz.**

1   The main difference between academic writing and normal writing is that academic writing:

   (a) uses longer words

   (b) tries to be precise and unbiased

   (c) is harder to understand

2   The difference between a project and an essay is:

   (a) essays are longer

   (b) projects are longer

   (c) students choose projects' topics

3   Teachers complain most about students:

   (a) not answering the question given

   (b) not writing enough

   (c) not referencing properly

4   The best time to write an introduction is often:

   (a) first

   (b) last

   (c) after writing the main body

5   Plagiarism is:

   (a) a dangerous disease

   (b) an academic offence

   (c) an academic website

6   Making careful notes is essential for:

     (a) writing essays

     (b) revising for exams

     (c) all academic work

7   An in-text citation looks like:

     (a) (Manton, 2008)

     (b) (Richard Manton, 2008)

     (c) (Manton, R. 2008)

8   Paraphrasing a text means:

     (a) making it shorter

     (b) changing a lot of the vocabulary

     (c) adding more detail

9   Paragraphs always contain:

     (a) six or more sentences

     (b) an example

     (c) a topic sentence

10   The purpose of an introduction is:

     (a) to give your aims and methods

     (b) to excite the reader

     (c) to summarise your ideas

11   Proof-reading means:

     (a) getting a friend to check your work

     (b) checking for minor errors

     (c) rewriting

12   Teachers expect students to adopt a critical approach to their
     sources:

     (a) sometimes

     (b) only for Master's work

     (c) always

Answers on p. 272.

The writing process

Background to writing

Most business schools assess students mainly through written assignments. These include coursework, which may take weeks to write, and exam answers, which may have to be written in an hour or less. Students need to be clear about the terms used to describe different types of assignments, and also about the basic components of each. This unit deals with both of these topics, and also introduces the use of sentences and paragraphs.

1 What is academic writing?

Although there is no fixed standard of academic writing, it is clearly different from the written style of newspapers or novels. Similarly, it is generally agreed that academic writing attempts to be accurate and objective. What are its other features?

■ Working alone or in a group, list your ideas below.

- _____
- _____
- _____
- _____

2 Common types of academic writing

Below are the most common types of written work produced by business students.

■ **Match the terms on the left to the definitions on the right.**

Notes	A piece of research, either individual or group work, with the topic chosen by the student(s).
Report	The longest piece of writing normally done by a student (20,000+ words) often for a higher degree, on a topic chosen by the student.
Project	A written record of the main points of a text or lecture, for a student's personal use.
Essay	A description of something a student has done e.g. conducting a survey.
Dissertation/ Thesis	The most common type of written work, with the title given by the teacher, normally 1000–5000 words.

3 The structure of academic texts

Short essays (including exam answers) generally have this pattern:

Introduction

Main body

Conclusion

Longer essays may include:

Introduction

Main body
    Literature review
    Case study
    Discussion

References
Conclusion
Appendices

▶ **See Unit 4.5 Writing longer essays**

Dissertations and journal articles may have:

Abstract
List of contents
List of tables
Introduction

Main body
    Literature review
    Case study
    Findings
    Discussion

Conclusion
Acknowledgements
References
Appendices

■ **Find the words in the lists above that match the following definitions:**

(a) A short summary of 100–200 words which explains the paper's purpose and main findings.

_____

(b) A list of all the sources the writer has mentioned in the text.

_____

(c) A section, at the end, where less important information is included.

_____

(d) A short section where people who have helped the writer are thanked.

_____

(e) Part of the main body in which the writer discusses relevant research.

_____

(f) A section where one particular example is described in detail.

_____

4 The format of academic writing

There is considerable variation in the format of academic writing required by different schools and departments. Your teachers may give you guidelines, or you should ask them what they want. But some general features apply to most formats.

■ **Look at the example below and identify the features underlined, using the words in the box below.**

sentence   heading   sub-title

paragraph   title   phrase

(a) **The Effectiveness of Microcredit**

(b) An evaluation of programmes in India and the Philippines.

(c) Introduction

(d) In the last ten years considerable claims have been made about the value of microcredit (also known as microfinance); the provision of unsecured small loans to the poor in

(e) developing countries. But it has proved surprisingly difficult to accurately measure the effectiveness of these loans, without interference from other non-commercial factors.

(f) Two recent studies have attempted to compare the effects on randomly-chosen groups of people with access to microcredit, compared to those without. The first (Bannerjee *et al.*, 2009), based at Massachusetts Institute of Technology (MIT), looked at slumdwellers in the city of Hyderabad in India, while the second (Karlan and Zinman, 2009) compared borrowers and non-borrowers in the Philippines. Overall, neither study found evidence that microcredit had any effect in reducing poverty, although it may have some other positive aspects such as reducing the consumption of alcohol or tobacco.

(a) _____

(b) _____

(c) _____

(d) _____

(e) _____

(f) _____

5 Other common text features

(a) **Reference** to sources:
   The first (Bannerjee et al., 2009) looked at slumdwellers . . .

(b) The use of **abbreviations** to save space:
   Massachusetts Institute of Technology (MIT)

(c) **Italics:** used to show words from other languages:
   Bannerjee *et al.* (= 'and others')

(d) **Brackets:** used to give subsidiary information or to clarify a point:
   (also known as microfinance)

(e) **Numbering systems:** (1.1, 1.2) are often used in reports, less so in essays.

6 Simple and complex sentences

■ **Study the table below.**

Annual vehicle production 2005–9

2005	2006	2007	2008	2009
135,470	156,935	164,820	159,550	123,075

All sentences contain verbs:

> In 2005 the company <u>produced</u> over 135,000 vehicles.
>
> Between 2005 and 2006 vehicle production <u>increased</u> by 20 per cent.

Simple sentences are easier to write and read, but complex sentences are also needed in academic writing. However, students should make clarity a priority, and avoid writing very complex sentences until they feel confident in their ability.

Complex sentences contain **conjunctions, relative pronouns** or **punctuation**, which link the clauses:

> In 2005 the company produced over 135,000 vehicles <u>but</u> between 2005 and 2006 production increased by 20 per cent.
>
> Over 164,000 vehicles were produced in 2007<u>;</u> by 2009 this had fallen to 123,000.

■ **Write two simple and two complex sentences using data from the table above.**

(a) _____

(b) _____

(c) _____

(d) _____

7 Writing in paragraphs

■ **Discuss the following questions:**

(a) What is a paragraph?

(b) Why are texts divided into paragraphs?

(c) How long are paragraphs?

■ **Read the Text 7.1 opposite and divide it into a suitable number of paragraphs.**

7.1 INVESTMENT STRATEGIES

Most people want to invest for the future, to cover unexpected financial difficulties and provide security. Different people, however, tend to have different requirements, so that a 25-year-old just leaving university would be investing for long-term capital growth, whereas a 60-year-old who had just retired would probably invest for income. Despite these differences, certain principles apply in most cases. The first issue to consider is risk. In general, the greater the degree of risk, the higher the return. Shares, for example, which can quickly rise or fall in value, typically have a higher yield than bonds, which offer greater stability. Therefore all investors must decide how much risk is appropriate in their particular situation. Diversification must also be considered in an investment strategy. Wise investors usually seek to spread their investments across a variety of geographical and business sectors. As accurate predictions of the future are almost impossible, it is best to have as many options as possible. A further consideration is investor involvement. Some investors opt for a high degree of involvement and want to buy and sell regularly, constantly watching the markets. But personal involvement can be time-consuming and worrying, and many prefer to leave the management of their portfolios to professional fund managers.

▶ **See Unit 1.10 Organising paragraphs**

Critical reading

Students often underestimate the importance of reading effectively, but good reading techniques are vital for success on any business course. This unit examines the most suitable text types for academic work, explores ways of locating relevant materials in the library, explains different reading methods, and introduces a critical approach to potential sources.

1 Academic texts

You need to read a variety of text types for your course, and it is important to identify suitable types and recognise their features. This will help you to assess their value.

■ **You are studying tourism marketing. Read the texts 1.1–1.4 below and decide which are the most suitable for academic use.**

Text	Suitability?
1	
2	
3	
4	

1.1   To promote tourism and market destination, it is important to study the tourists' attitude, behaviour and demand. The studies of Levitt (1986) and Kotler and Armstrong (1994) suggest that an understanding of consumer behaviour may help with the marketing planning process in tourism marketing. The research of consumer behaviour is the key to the underpinning of all marketing activity which is carried out to develop, promote and sell tourism products (Swarbrooke and Horner, 1999; Asad, 2005). Therefore, the study of consumer behaviour has become necessary for the sake of tourism marketing.

1.2   The romance of travel has always fascinated me, and our recent trip to Thailand lived up to expectations. We flew from Gatwick and after a comfortable flight arrived in Bangkok just as the sun was rising. Our stay in the city lasted only a couple of days before we set off for the hill country around Chang Mai, where we were planning to visit some of the indigenous tribes who live in this mountainous region. When we arrived the weather was rather disappointing, but after a day the heavy rain gave way to sparkling clear sunshine.

1.3   Holiday trips to the Antarctica have quadrupled in the past decade and last year more than 46,000 people visited the land mass and surrounding oceans. However, safety fears and concerns about the impact visitors are having on the delicate frozen landscape have soared and members of the Antarctic Treaty–an agreement between 28 nations, including the UK, on the use of the continent–are now meeting to discuss ways to regulate tourism.

British officials are seeking to establish a 'strategic agreement for tourism' around the South Pole. If successful, it will see treaty members introduce new measures to improve the safety of tourist trips, while also reducing the impact that visitors will have on the environment. The regulations could see limits on the number of ships and landings, restrictions on how close they come to shore, a ban on building tourist facilities and hotels on the continent, and rules on waste discharges from ships.

1.4   Equally, from a political perspective, the nature of state involvement in and policies for tourism is dependent on both the political-economic structures and the prevailing political ideology in the destination state, with comparisons typically made between market-led and centrally planned economies. For example, the Thatcher–Reagan-inspired neo-liberalism of the 1980s, and the subsequent focus on privatisation and the markets in many Western nations contrasted starkly with the then centrally planned tourism sectors in the former Eastern Europe (Buckley and Witt, 1990; Hall, 1991). At the same time, of course, it has also long been recognised that the political-economic relationship of one nation with another or with the wider international community (that is, the extent of political-economic dependency) may represent a significant influence on tourism development (Telfer, 2002). Thus, in short, tourism planning and development in the destination tends to reflect both the structures and political ideologies of the state and its international political-economic relations.

■   Decide what are main features of academic texts. List them in the table below, with examples from the texts above.

Feature	Example
1 *Formal vocabulary*	*The marketing planning process in tourism marketing ... the extent of political-economic dependency ...*
2	
3	
4	

2 Types of text

■ **Think of all the various types of text that you might need to read for your course. List them in the table below, with their likely advantages and disadvantages.**

Text type	Advantage	Disadvantage
1 *Textbook*	*Written for students*	*May be out of date*
2		
3		
4		
5		
6		

3 Using reading lists

Your teacher may give you a printed reading list, or it may be available online through the library website. The list will usually include textbooks, journal articles and websites. If the list is electronic there will be links to the library catalogue to let you check on the availability of the material. If the list is printed, you will have to use the library catalogue to find the texts.

You do not have to read every word of a book because it is on the list. Your teacher will probably suggest which pages to read, and also tell you what your priorities should be.

On reading lists you will find the following formats:

Books
> 'The European Workforce: Change and Regulation', (2001)
> Chapter 6 in S. Mercado, R. Welford and K. Prescott, *European Business*, Fourth Edition, Prentice Hall, London, pp. 203–247

Journal articles
> W. Mayrhofer and C. Brewster (1996) 'In Praise of Ethnocentricity: Expatriate Policies in European Multinationals', *The International Executive* 38(6), 749–778

Websites
> http://europa.eu/pol/socio/index_en.htm

4 Using library catalogues

University and college libraries usually have online catalogues. These allow students to search for the materials they want in various ways. If the title and author's name are known it is easy to check if the book is available. But if you are making a search for material on a specific topic you may have to vary the search terms. For instance, if you want information about exploration for oil, you might try:

> Oil exploration
>
> Exploring for oil
>
> Hydrocarbon exploration
>
> Exploring for hydrocarbons

■ You have been given an essay title: 'Outline the current state of global exploration for oil, and relate this to future levels of production'.

■ You have entered the term 'oil exploration' in the library catalogue search engine, and these are the seven results. Which would you select to borrow? Give your reasons.

Full details	Title	Edn/ year	Location	Holdings
1	Hydrocarbon Exploration and Production/by Frank Jahn, Mark Cook and Mark Graham.	2nd ed. 2008	Science Library	Availability
2	China and the Global Energy Crisis: Development and Prospects for China's Oil and Natural Gas/Tatsu Kambara, Christopher Howe.	2007	Main Library	Availability
3	Deepwater Petroleum Exploration and Production [electronic resource]: A Non-technical Guide/William L. Leffler, Richard Pattarozzi, Gordon Sterling.	2003	Main Library	Availability
4	Soft Computing and Intelligent Data Analysis in Oil Exploration [electronic resource]/edited by M. Nikravesh, F. Aminzadeh, L.A. Zadeh	2003	Main Library	Availability
5	Operational Aspects of Oil and Gas Well Testing [electronic resource]/Stuart McAleese.	2000	Main Library	Availability
6	Oil and Gas Exploration in Derbyshire.	198-?	History Library	Availability
7	Geophysical Exploration: An Outline of the Principal Methods used in the search for Minerals, Oil, Gas and Water Supplies/F.W. Dunning.	1970	Science Library	Availability

Full details
If you click on this you will get more information about the book, including the number of pages and a summary of the contents. This may help you decide whether to borrow it.

Location
Many large universities have more than one library. This tells you which one the book is kept in.

Holdings
If you click on availability it will tell you how many copies the library holds and if they are available to borrow or out on loan.

5 Using library websites to search electronic resources

E-journals and other electronic resources such as subject databases are becoming increasingly important. Their advantage is that they can be accessed by computer, saving the need to visit the library and find a text. Most library websites have a separate portal or gateway for searching electronic resources. This allows you to enter the name of a specific journal, or look for possible journals in your subject area by entering a term such as 'international business law'. In this case, the database may offer the following titles:

European Business Law Review

European Business Organisation Law Review

International Trade and Business Law Review

Law and Business Review of the Americas

In each case, you can access a list of issues available, which will let you read a list of published articles. In the case of *European Business Organisation Law Review*, the list would include:

Dec 2009 Vol. 10 Issue 4

Sep 2009 Vol. 10 Issue 3

June 2009 Vol. 10 Issue 2

Mar 2009 Vol. 10 Issue 1

By clicking on any of these issues you can read a full list of articles. It is usually sufficient to read the abstract to find out if the article will be relevant to your work. Note that most journal websites contain a search engine to allow you to search all back issues by subject. They may also offer links to articles in other journals on the same topic.

The best way to become familiar with these methods is to practise. Library websites usually contain tutorials for new students, and librarians are always willing to give help and advice when needed.

6 Reading methods

It is easy for students to underestimate the importance of reading skills. Especially for international students, reading academic texts in the quantity required for most courses is a demanding task. But students will not benefit from attending lectures and seminars unless the reading is done promptly, while clearly most writing tasks require extensive reading.

Moreover, the texts often contain new vocabulary and phrases, and may be written in a rather formal style. This means that distinct methods have to be adopted to cope with the volume of reading required, which is especially important when you are reading in another language. Clearly, you do not have time to read every word published on the topic you are studying. The chart below illustrates an approach to finding and dealing with texts.

■ **Complete the empty boxes in the chart with the following techniques:**

- read intensively to make notes on key points

- scan text for information you need (e.g. names)

- survey text features (e.g. abstract, contents, index)

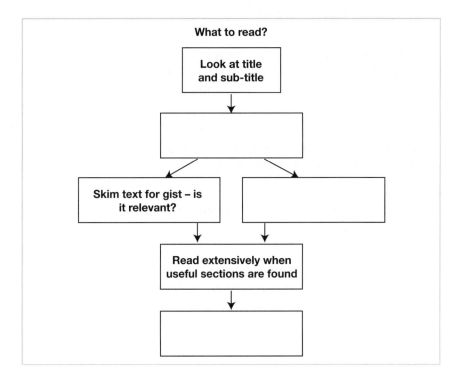

(a) What is the difference between skimming and scanning?

(b) Can you suggest any other reading skills to add to the chart above?

7 Titles, sub-titles and text features

Many books and articles have both a title and a sub-title:

> Much Ado about Nothing? Do domestic firms really benefit
> from foreign direct investment?

The title is usually shorter; the sub-title often gives more information
about the focus.

After finding a relevant text, it is worth checking the following text features
before starting to read:

Author
Is the writer well-known in his/her field? What else has he/she
published?

Publication date and edition
Normally you need to read up-to-date texts. Do not use a first
edition if there is a (revised) second edition available.

Abstract
All journal articles have an abstract, which is a paragraph
summarising the purpose and conclusions of the article. Reading
this should give you a good idea of the relevance of the text for
you.

Contents
A list of the main chapters or sections. This should tell you how
much space is devoted to the topic you are researching.

Introduction or preface
This is where the author often explains his/her reasons for writing,
and also how the text is organised.

References
This list shows all the sources used by the author and referred to
in the text. It may give you some suggestions for further reading.

Bibliography
These are the sources the author has used but not specifically
referred to.

Index
An alphabetical list of all the topics and names mentioned in a book.
If, for example, you are looking for information about a person, the
index will tell you if that person is mentioned, and how often.

8 Assessing texts critically

You cannot afford to waste time on texts that are unreliable or out-of-date. If you are using material that is not on the reading list you must assess it critically to ensure that the writer can be trusted and the material is trustworthy.

■ (a) Compare these two texts on a pharmaceutical company. Which is the more reliable?

8.1   Our success is based on a commitment to discovery, finding new ideas that are inspired by life and which in turn help to inspire the lives of our stakeholders. We discover new medicines that are designed to improve the health and quality of life of patients around the world – medicines which are innovative, effective and which offer added benefits such as reduced side effects or better ways of taking the treatment. We also focus on getting the best from every medicine we make by exploring all the ways it can be used or improved. With a global business comes a global responsibility for consistently high standards of behaviour worldwide. We aim to effectively manage that responsibility and help to find new ways of bringing benefit to society to ensure that Medmax continues to be welcomed as a valued member of the global community.

8.2   Recent trading results from Medmax show an apparently healthy position, with pre-tax profit rising by 24 per cent and total revenues up 5 per cent. These figures, however, were inflated by some one-off gains, such as a $152 million sale of swine flu vaccine to the US government. Sales of the ZX high blood pressure drug also increased sharply due to its main rival being temporarily off the market due to safety concerns. Costs were very significantly lower in the last quarter, falling 14 per cent, due to productivity improvements. The anti-cholesterol drug Somar also sold very well, becoming the market leader, but there are concerns that a pending US court case may soon challenge Medmax's patent on this product. There are also worries that re-organisation of the American healthcare system may affect Medmax's long-term profits, and the company's shares have recently fallen by 6 per cent.

The first text contains little or no precise information about the company's performance and is full of statements that cannot be checked (medicines that are innovative, effective . . .). It appears to be taken from the company website. By contrast the second seems to be based on a recent financial report and contains both facts (profits rising by 24 per cent) and some comment (may affect Medmax's long-term profits). The first text is of little use to a student, the second could be used, with care, for analysis of the company's current state.

■ **(b) Read the following texts and decide if they are reliable or not. Give reasons for your decisions in the table below.**

8.3   Hard up? Why struggle when you could live in luxury? Solve your money worries easily and quickly by working for us. No experience needed, you can earn hundreds of pounds for just a few hours' work per day. Work when it suits you, day or night. Don't delay, call today for an interview on 07795–246791.

8.4   If you have money problems, there's lots of ways you can save cash. Instead of spending money on new clothes, try buying them second-hand from charity shops, where you'll find lots of stylish bargains. Eating out is another big expense, but instead you can get together with a few friends and cook a meal together; it's cheaper and it's fun. Bus fares and taxis can also cost a lot, so it might be worth looking for a cheap bicycle, which lets you travel where you want, when you want.

8.5   Most students find that they have financial difficulties at times. It has been estimated that nearly 55 per cent experience financial difficulties in their first year at college or university. It's often hard living on a small fixed income, and the cost of accommodation and food can come as a shock when you first live away from your parents. The most important thing, if you find you are getting into debt, is to speak to a financial advisor in the Student Union, who may be able to help you sort out your problems.

1	
2	
3	

■ (c) You are writing an essay on diversification in business. You find the following article in a recent magazine. Read it critically and decide whether you could use it in your work.

8.6 **CHANGE ON THE FARM**

In the last 20 years the structure of British farming has changed significantly. Many small farms have been merged to create fewer mega-farms, with all the benefits of scale. But another important development has been to increase the income obtained from activities other than growing food. In Earlswood, Warwickshire a farmer has created a three-hectare 'maize maze' which over 15,000 people have paid £5 to explore during the summer. This more than compensates for the cost of designing and cutting the attraction. In the autumn, over 80 per cent of the maize should still be saleable as cattle feed, giving the farmer a double income. Such enterprises are examples of the new 'agritainment' sector, along with bed-and-breakfast accommodation, shooting ranges and wedding venues.

The Department for the Environment, Food and Rural Affairs (DEFRA) estimates that over 10 per cent of farms have diversified their income by offering recreational activities, and over 15 per cent of farm income is now derived from such sources. This has provided farmers with a cushion against the swings of commodity prices in the last few years, although with the current rise in global food prices farmers may be becoming less interested in converting their old barns into craft workshops.

(a) Positive aspects:

_____

(b) Negative aspects:

_____

9 Critical thinking

Even when you feel that a text is reliable and that you can safely use it as a source, it is still important to adopt a critical attitude towards it. This approach is perhaps easiest to learn when reading, but is important for all other academic work (i.e. listening, discussing and writing). Critical thinking means not just passively accepting what you hear or read, but instead actively questioning and assessing it. As you read you should ask yourself the following questions:

(a) What are the key ideas in this?

(b) Does the thesis of the writer develop logically, step by step?

(c) Are the examples given helpful? Would other examples be better?

(d) Does the author have any bias?

(e) Does the evidence presented seem reliable?

(f) Is this argument similar to anything else I have read?

(g) Do I agree with the writer's views?

■ **Read the following text (9.1), thinking critically about the sections in bold. Then answer questions 1–9.**

1   '. . . **such as the invention of fire, pottery and the telephone'**

Are these really critical developments?

2   '. . . **the development of the internet is perhaps the most crucial of all'**

Is this true?

3   '. . . **so that few people can imagine life without it** '

Can I imagine living without the internet?

4   '**It is estimated that over 70 per cent of North Americans, for instance, have internet access'**

No source given. Does this figure seem likely?

5   '**Physical shops are under threat, as growing numbers shop online'**

Is the first part true, and if so, is it caused by online shopping?

9.1 THE GROWTH OF THE WORLD WIDE WEB

In the history of civilization there have been many significant developments, **such as the invention of fire, pottery and the telephone,** but **the development of the internet is perhaps the most crucial of all.** In the space of a few years the world wide web has linked buyers in New York to sellers in Mumbai and teachers in Berlin to students in Cairo, **so that few people can imagine life without it.**

It is estimated that over 70 per cent of North Americans, for instance, have internet access, and these figures are steadily increasing. **Physical shops are under threat, as growing numbers shop online.** In areas such as travel it is now impossible to buy tickets on certain airlines except on the internet. The web also links together millions of individual traders who sell to buyers through websites such as Ebay.

Beyond the commercial sphere, the internet is also critically important in the academic world. A huge range of journals and reports are now available electronically, meaning that researchers can access a vast amount of information through their computer screens, **speeding up their work and allowing them to produce better quality research.** In addition, email permits academics to make effortless contact with fellow-researchers all over the world, which also assists them to improve their output.

There is, of course, a darker side to this phenomenon, which is the use criminals have made of their ability to trade illegal or fraudulent products over the internet, with little control over their activities. But such behaviour is hugely compensated for by the benefits that have been obtained by both individuals and businesses. **We are reaching a situation in which all kinds of information are freely available to everyone, which must lead to a happier, healthier and richer society.**

6   '. . . speeding up their work and allowing them to produce
    better quality research'

    If the first part is true, does the result logically follow?

7   'We are reaching a situation in which all kinds of information
    are freely available to everyone, which must lead to a happier,
    healthier and richer society'

    Does the first part need any qualification?

    Is the conclusion justified?

8   Is the writer objective or biased?

9   Do I agree with this argument overall?

▶ See Unit 2.1 Argument and discussion.

Avoiding plagiarism

In the English-speaking academic world it is essential to use a wide range of sources for your writing and to acknowledge these sources clearly. This unit explains why this is vital, and introduces the techniques students need to use. Further practice with these is provided in Units 1.6 Paraphrasing, 1.7 Summarising and 1.8 References and quotations.

1 What is plagiarism?

Plagiarism is a topic that has generated a lot of debate. Basically it means taking ideas or words from a source without giving credit (acknowledgement). In academic work, ideas and words are seen as private property belonging to the person who first thought or wrote them. If you borrow or refer to the work of another person, you must show that you have done this by providing the correct acknowledgement. This is done by the following methods:

Summary and citation
Rodgers (2007) argues that family-owned businesses survive recessions better.

Quotation and citation
As Rodgers maintains: 'There is strong evidence for the resilience of family businesses in recessionary times.' (Rodgers, 2007: 23)

These citations are linked to a list of **references** at the end of the main text, which would include the following details:

Author	Date	Title	Place of publication	Publisher
Rodgers, F.	(2007)	*The Family Business: A Re-assessment*	Oxford	Critchlow

This reference gives the reader the necessary information to find the source if more detail is required. The citations make it clear to the reader that you have read Rodgers and borrowed this idea from him. Not to do this is seen as a kind of theft, and as such is considered to be an academic crime. Therefore it is important for all students, including international ones, to understand the meaning of plagiarism and learn how to prevent it in their work.

▶ **See Unit 1.8 References and quotations.**

2 Degrees of plagiarism

Although plagiarism essentially means copying somebody else's work, it is not always easy to define.

■ **Working with a partner, consider the academic situations in the following table (p. 27) and decide if they are plagiarism.**

Students who plagiarise often do so accidentally. For example, situation (10), when the author's name is mis-spelt, is technically plagiarism but really carelessness. In situation (9) your teacher may have encouraged you to discuss the topic in groups, and then write an essay on your own, in which case it would not be plagiarism. Self-plagiarism is also theoretically possible, as in situation (7). It can also be difficult to decide what is general or common knowledge, situation (6), but you can always try asking colleagues.

However, it is not a good excuse to say that you didn't know the rules of plagiarism, or that you didn't have time to write in your own words. Nor is it adequate to say that the rules are different in your own country. In general, anything that is not common knowledge or your own ideas and research (published or not) must be cited and referenced.

	Situation	Yes/No
1	Copying a paragraph, but changing a few words and giving a citation.	
2	Cutting and pasting a short article from a website, with no citation.	
3	Taking two paragraphs from a classmate's essay, without citation.	
4	Taking a graph from a textbook, giving the source.	
5	Taking a quotation from a source, giving a citation but not using quotation marks.	
6	Using an idea that you think of as general knowledge, e.g. the Great Depression was caused by restrictions on free trade, without citation.	
7	Using a paragraph from an essay you wrote and had marked the previous semester, without citation.	
8	Using the results of your own research, e.g. from a survey, without citation.	
9	Discussing an essay topic with a group of classmates and using some of their ideas in your own work.	
10	Giving a citation for some information but mis-spelling the author's name.	

3 Summarising and paraphrasing

Quotations should not be over-used, so you must learn to paraphrase and summarise in order to include other writers' ideas in your work. Paraphrasing involves rewriting a text so that the language is substantially different while the content stays the same, while summarising means reducing the length of a text but retaining the main points. Paraphrasing is practised in Unit 1.6, and summarising in Unit 1.7.

Normally both skills are used at the same time, as can be seen in the examples below.

■ **Read the following text and then compare the five paragraphs below, which borrow ideas and information. Decide which are plagiarised and which are acceptable, and give your reasons in the table below.**

3.1   RAILWAY MANIAS

In 1830 there were a few dozen miles of railways in all the world – chiefly consisting of the line from Liverpool to Manchester. By 1840 there were over 4,500 miles, by 1850 over 23,500. Most of them were projected in a few bursts of speculative frenzy known as the 'railway manias' of 1835–7 and especially in 1844–7; most of them were built in large part with British capital, British iron, machines and know-how. These investment booms appear irrational, because in fact few railways were much more profitable to the investor than other forms of enterprise, most yielded quite modest profits and many none at all: in 1855 the average interest on capital sunk in the British railways was a mere 3.7 per cent. (From *The Age of Revolution* by Eric Hobsbawm, 1995, p. 45.)

(a) Between 1830 and 1850 there was very rapid development in railway construction world wide. Two periods of especially feverish growth were 1835–7 and 1844–7. It is hard to understand the reason for this intense activity, since railways were not particularly profitable investments and some produced no return at all. (Hobsbawm, 1995, 45)

(b) There were only a few dozen miles of railways in 1830, including the Liverpool to Manchester line. But by 1840 there were over 4,500 miles and over 23,500 by 1850. Most of them were built in large part with British capital, British iron, machines and know-how, and most of them were projected in a few bursts of speculative frenzy known as the 'railway manias' of 1835–7 and especially in 1844–7. Because most yielded quite modest profits and many none at all these investment booms appear irrational. In fact few railways were much more profitable to the investor than other forms of enterprise. (Hobsbawm, 1995, 45)

(c) As Hobsbawm (1995) argues, nineteenth-century railway mania was partly irrational: 'because in fact few railways were much more profitable to the investor than other forms of enterprise, most yielded quite modest profits and many none at all: in 1855 the average interest on capital sunk in the British railways was a mere 3.7 per cent.' (Hobsbawm, 1995, 45)

(d) Globally, railway networks increased dramatically from 1830 to 1850; the majority in short periods of 'mania' (1835–7 and 1844–7). British technology and capital were responsible for much of this growth, yet the returns on the investment were hardly any better than comparable business opportunities. (Hobsbawm, 1895, 45)

(e) The dramatic growth of railways between 1830 and 1850 was largely achieved using British technology. However, it has been claimed that much of this development was irrational because few railways were much more profitable to the investor than other forms of enterprise; most yielded quite modest profits and many none at all.

	Plagiarised or acceptable?
a	
b	
c	
d	
e	

From understanding titles to planning

In both exams and coursework it is essential for students to understand what an essay title is asking them to do. A plan can then be drawn up, which should prevent time being wasted, while ensuring the question is answered fully. This unit looks at some key words in titles and presents alternative methods of essay planning.

1 The planning process

Essay planning is necessary in all academic situations, but clearly there are important differences between planning in exams, when time is short, and for coursework, when preparatory reading is required. However, the process of planning should include these steps in both cases:

(a) Analyse the title wording and decide what is required.

(b) Brainstorm the topic to focus your ideas.

(c) Prepare an outline using your preferred method.

Teachers frequently complain that students do not answer the question set, but this problem can be avoided by more care at the planning stage.

2 Essay titles

Titles contain key words, which tell the student what to do. Note that titles often have two (or more) parts:

> **What** is meant by a demand curve and **why** would we expect it to slope downwards?

In this case, 'what' is asking for a description and 'why' for a reason or explanation.

■ **Underline the key words in the following titles and consider what they are asking you to do.**

(a) How and why has the market for international tourism segmented since the middle of the twentieth century? What are the economic and social forces that have driven this process?

(b) 'The internet has rendered obsolete the traditional theories of the internationalisation of firms.' Critically evaluate this statement.

(c) Describe the barriers and challenges to managing diversity and critically examine organisational practices.

(d) Discuss the relationship between knowledge and power in organisations. Consider the implications for managers.

3 Practice exercise: Essay titles

■ **Look at the table on the following page and match the key words on the left to the definitions on the right.**

4 Brainstorming

It is often helpful to start thinking about a topic by writing down any ideas you have, in any order. Taking the example from (2a) above, you might collect the points shown in Box 4.1 on the following page.

1 Analyse	Explain a topic briefly and clearly
2 Assess (Evaluate)	Deal with a complex subject by reducing it to the main elements
3 Describe	Divide into sections and discuss each critically/consider widely
4 Discuss	Break down into the various parts and their relationships
5 Examine (Explore)	Make a proposal and support it
6 Illustrate	Look at various aspects of a topic, compare benefits and drawbacks
7 Outline (Trace)	Give a detailed account of something
8 State	Give a simple, basic account of the main points of a topic
9 Suggest	Give examples
10 Summarise	Decide the value or worth of a subject

4.1 INTERNATIONAL TOURISM – SEGMENTATION OF MARKET

How and why:
- Package holidays made foreign holidays popular
- Internet allows travellers to plan own holidays
- In '60s jet aircraft permit faster travel – long and short haul holidays
- In '90s budget airlines lower costs – short breaks

Economic and political forces:
- Rising disposable incomes permit more spending on travel
- Developing countries see tourism as route to growth
- Older, retired people spend more on travel

■ **Brainstorm ideas for title (5a) below:**

> *Describe the typical social, cultural and environmental impacts experienced by tourist destinations in developing countries. How can harmful impacts be reduced or avoided?*

5 Essay length

Coursework essays usually have a required length, normally between 1,000 and 5,000 words. You must keep to this limit, although deviations of 5 per cent more or less are generally acceptable. However, at the planning stage you need to consider what proportion of the essay to allocate to each part of the question.

As a basic guide, 20 per cent is usually sufficient for the introduction and conclusion together (references are not included in the word count). Therefore, in a 2,000-word essay the main body would have 1,600 words.

If this was the length given for title (2a) above, you might decide on the following allocation:

Segmentation of the market for international tourism – how	300 words
– why	500 words
Economic forces	400 words
Social forces	400 words

This calculation is useful since it can guide the amount of reading you need to do, as well as providing the basis for an outline. Moreover, it prevents you from writing an unbalanced answer, in which part of the question is not fully developed.

Essays in exams do not have a word limit, but it is equally important to plan them in similar terms, e.g. part 1, 40 per cent, part 2, 60 per cent.

■ **Identify the key words in the following titles and decide what percentage of the main body to give to each part.**

(a) Describe the typical social, cultural and environmental impacts experienced by tourist destinations in developing countries. How can harmful impacts be reduced or avoided?

(b) 'Monopolies are inefficient in using resources.' Explain and discuss.

(c) What problems do East Asian businesses face in integrating with the global economy? Discuss with reference to a country example.

6 Outlines

An outline should help the writer to answer the question as effectively as possible. Care at this stage will save wasted effort later. The more detail you include in your outline, the easier the writing process will be. Note that for coursework it is usually better to write the main body first, then the introduction and finally the conclusion. Therefore you may prefer to outline just the main body at this stage.

There is no fixed pattern for an outline; different methods appeal to different students. Take the first part of title (5a) above: 'Describe the typical social, cultural and environmental impacts experienced by tourist destinations in developing countries.'

(a) The outline might be a list:

  (i)   Social impacts

   •   increase in variety of jobs available
   •   price inflation
   •   new range of business opportunities

   (ii)   Cultural impacts

- new patterns of dress and behaviour may cause problems
- market for traditional crafts and/or rituals grows

  (iii) Environmental impacts

- increased pressure on limited resources, e.g. water
- loss of natural habitat to building projects
- provision of new infrastructure, e.g. roads

(b) An alternative is a mind map:

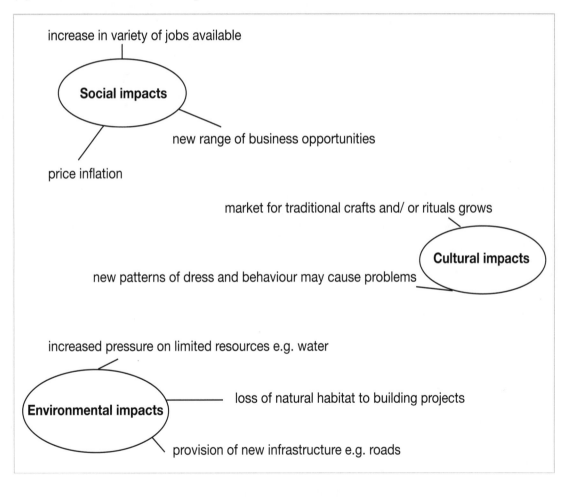

◼ **(c) What are the advantages and drawbacks of each method?**

■ (d) Prepare an outline for the second part of the same title: 'How can harmful impacts be reduced or avoided?'

Outline

Finding key points and note-making

After finding a suitable source and identifying relevant sections of text, the next step is to select the key points that relate to your topic and make notes on them. This unit explains and practises this process, which also involves skills developed in Units 1.6 Paraphrasing and 1.7 Summarising.

1 Note-making

■ **What are the main reasons for note-making? Add to the list below.**

(a) To prepare for essay writing

(b) _____

(c) _____

(d) _____

(e) _____

2 Note-making methods

You are looking for information on the current media revolution.

■ Study the text below (key points underlined) and the notes in the box. What do you notice about the language of the notes?

2.1   **THE DEATH OF THE PRESS?**

A hundred years ago news was exclusively provided by newspapers. There was no other way of supplying the latest information on politics, crime, finance or sport to the millions of people who bought and read newspapers, sometimes twice a day. Today the situation is very different. The same news is also available on television, radio and the internet, and because of the nature of these media, can be more up-to-date than in print. For young people, especially, the internet has become the natural source of news and comment.

This development means that in many countries newspaper circulation is falling, and a loss of readers also means a fall in advertising, which is the main income for most papers. Consequently, in both Britain and the USA newspapers are closing every week. But when a local newspaper goes out of business an important part of the community is lost. It allows debate on local issues, as well as providing a noticeboard for events such as weddings and society meetings.

All newspapers are concerned by these developments, and many have tried to find methods of increasing their sales. One approach is to focus on magazine-type articles rather than news, another is to give free gifts such as DVDs, while others have developed their own websites to provide continuous news coverage. However, as so much is now freely available online to anyone with a web browser, none of these have had a significant impact on the steady decline of paid-for newspapers.

Source: *New Business Monthly*, May 2010, p. 37

Decline of newspapers   (*New Business Monthly*, May 2010, p. 37)

a)   Newspapers only source of news 100 yrs ago – now also TV, radio + www

b)   Newspaper sales   ⟍⟍⟍⟍⟍→   > decline in advertising > newspapers shutting

c)   Attempts to increase sales: – more magazine content
                                        – gifts
                                        – websites

                  but none effective.

---

3 Practice exercise: Finding key points

■   Read the following text and underline two key points. Then choose a
    title for it.

> **3.1**   The generation born after the Second World War,
>   sometimes called the baby-boomers, are now reaching
> retirement age, and businesses are starting to realise that they
> are a wealthier market than any previous retirement group.
> Financial products, travel and medicines are well-established
> industries which interest the over-60s, but others are now
> focusing on this age group. Volkswagen, for instance, has
> produced a car with raised seats and more interior space to
> appeal to their tastes. In Japan, with its ageing population,
> companies have more experience of selling to the retired, and
> have been successful with unusual products such as a robotic
> seal, which serves as a pet substitute for the lonely. There are,
> however, certain difficulties in selling to this market. Some
> customers resent being addressed as 'old' since they see
> themselves as more youthful, while there is a huge variation in
> the profile of the baby-boomers, ranging from healthy and
> active to the bed-ridden and infirm.

4 Relevance

When preparing to write an essay you have to search for information and ideas relevant to your subject. Therefore the key points that you select must relate to that topic.

You are given an essay title: 'Taxation: an instrument of social policy – Discuss.'

■ **Read the following article and underline the key points that relate to your essay topic.**

4.1 CAN TAXATION REDUCE OBESITY?

Taxation has been imposed by governments for thousands of years, and initially the basis of taxation was something easily assessed, such as land, hearths or windows, all of which were difficult to hide from the tax collector. But in more recent times governments have sought to use taxes not just to raise revenue, but also to reward virtue and discourage vice.

The practice of imposing taxes on products which are thought to have a negative social impact, such as alcohol, has been accepted for several hundred years, and are now called Pigouvian taxes (after the twentieth-century economist Arthur Pigou). Tobacco, gambling and carbon taxes are common examples. It has recently been suggested in the USA that so-called junk food should be taxed in order to compensate for the social costs of the obesity it is believed to cause. This proposal is based on the estimate of the medical costs of obesity, which is thought to be linked to cancer, diabetes and heart disease. These costs are shared by all taxpayers, not just the obese, so it is claimed that taxing items such as hamburgers and sugary drinks would both reduce consumption and help pay for medical care.

A study of the long-term effects of changes in food prices (Goldman, Lakdawalla and Zheng, 2009) argues that significant changes in consumption, and hence obesity levels, can be achieved over the long term. They claim that raising the price of calories by 10 per cent could eliminate nearly half the increase in obesity over a 20-year span. But the link between junk food and ill-health is not easily determined. A physically active person could eat hamburgers daily and still keep

continued . . .

> *cont.*   slim. In this respect it is quite different from drinking alcohol or causing air
> pollution.
>
> It has even been suggested that such a 'fat tax' might have the opposite effect and
> reduce activity levels by forcing people to spend more time preparing food for
> themselves, instead of buying it from fast-food outlets (Yaniv, Rosin and Tobol,
> 2009). Additionally, other studies on the effects of alcohol and tobacco taxes
> indicate that the heaviest users of these products are the least influenced by price
> rises, so that raising the price of hamburgers may do little to curb consumption
> among the most avid consumers. As these are often also the poorest, the tax
> would not only fail to improve their health, but would be regressive, making them
> even poorer.
>
> Source: Rohan, J. (2010), *Public Health Review* 8, p. 36

5 Effective note-making

Notes are for your personal use and you should create your own style.

(a) You must use your own words and not copy phrases from the
    original to avoid the risk of plagiarism. The quantity of notes you
    make depends on your task: you may only need a few points, or a lot
    of detail.

(b) Always record the source of your notes, to save time when you have
    to write the list of references.

(c) Notes are written quickly, so keep them simple. Do not write sentences.
    Leave out articles (a/the) and prepositions (of/to).

(d) If you write lists, it is important to have clear headings (underlined)
    and numbering systems (a, b, c, or 1, 2, 3,) to organise the information.
    Do not crowd your notes.

(e) Use symbols (+, >, =) to save time.

(f) Use abbreviations (e.g. = for example). You need to make up your
    own abbreviations for your subject area. But do not abbreviate too
    much, or you may find your notes hard to understand in the future!

▶ **See Unit 3.1 Abbreviations**

6 Practice exercise: Note-making

■ Complete the set of notes for 'Can taxation reduce obesity?' using the
key points underlined in (4) above.

Source: Rohan, J. (2010), Public Health Review 8, p. 36

Taxing junk food

1) *Goods > social harm e.g. alcohol have been taxed since 18th C.*

2) *US proposal to tax junk food – reduce obesity (medical costs – diabetes,
   heart disease)*

3)

4)

5)

6)

---

7 Practice exercise: Finding key points and note-making

You have to write an essay titled: 'What is the value of anti-monopoly
legislation?'

■ Read the following text and make notes on the relevant key points.

7.1 THE DIFFICULTY OF ASSESSING PREDATORY PRICING

Small companies often feel that larger rivals want to put them out of business by
discounting, for example the corner shop which cannot match the supermarket's
bargain offers. In 1890 the United States passed the Sherman Antitrust Act, which
was an attempt to prevent large companies exploiting their semi-monopoly
position, and many countries have adopted similar legislation. This is a response

---

continued . . .

cont.   to concerns that big businesses will lower prices to drive competitors to bankruptcy, and then be able to raise prices at will.

But clearly low prices are an advantage to consumers, and proving predation in court is a difficult process. Firms may have legitimate reasons for selling below cost, such as promoting a new product or because they expect their costs to fall when volume increases. In these cases current losses can be offset against future profits. Bundling goods, i.e. selling two or more products as a package, makes it even harder to establish malpractice. This is because the profit margin on each item in the bundle may vary. So a company that makes little profit on printers may sell them with higher profit margin ink cartridges. By doing this it can claim that other costs are being saved, for example on distribution.

In May 2009 the European Union found the chip-maker Intel guilty of predatory pricing against a rival, AMD, and fined the company 1.06 billion euros, claiming that European consumers of computers had suffered as a result of Intel providing incentives to manufacturers to favour its chips. But Intel appealed against the verdict, and the complexity of the case (the court verdict ran to over 500 pages) is an example of the difficulty of policing companies in this area.

Source: Caballero J. and Poledna Z. (2010), *European Business Prospects*, London: University Press, p. 351

Predatory pricing

Paraphrasing

Paraphrasing means changing the wording of a text so that it is significantly different from the original source, without changing the meaning. Effective paraphrasing is a key academic skill needed to avoid the risk of plagiarism, and to demonstrate your understanding of a source. This unit focuses on techniques for paraphrasing as part of the note-making and summarising process.

1 The elements of effective paraphrasing

Paraphrasing and summarising are normally used together in essay writing, but while summarising aims to reduce a source to an appropriate length, paraphrasing attempts to restate the relevant information. For example, the following sentence:

> There has been much debate about the reasons for the industrial revolution happening in eighteenth-century Britain, rather than in France or Germany.

could be paraphrased:

> Why the industrial revolution occurred in Britain in the eighteenth century, instead of on the continent, has been the subject of considerable discussion.

Note that an effective paraphrase usually:

- has a different structure to the original

- has mainly different vocabulary

- retains the same meaning

- keeps some phrases from the original that are in common use e.g. 'industrial revolution' or 'eighteenth century'

2 Practice exercise: Paraphrasing

■ Read the text below, and then decide which of the three paraphrases (a–c) is best.

2.1 **THE CAUSES OF THE INDUSTRIAL REVOLUTION**

Allen (2009) argues that the best explanation for the British location of the industrial revolution is found by studying demand factors. By the early eighteenth century high wages and cheap energy were both features of the British economy. Consequently, the mechanisation of industry through such inventions as the steam engine and mechanical spinning was profitable because employers were able to economise on labour by spending on coal. At that time, no other country had this particular combination of expensive labour and abundant fuel.

(a) A focus on demand may help explain the UK origin of the industrial revolution. At that time workers' pay was high, but energy from coal was inexpensive. This encouraged the development of inventions such as steam power, which enabled bosses to save money by mechanising production (Allen, 2009).

(b) The reason why Britain was the birthplace of the industrial revolution can be understood by analysing demand in the early 1700s, according to Allen (2009). He maintains that, uniquely, Britain had the critical combination of cheap energy from coal and high labour costs. This encouraged the adoption of steam power to mechanise production, thus saving on wages and increasing profitability.

(c) Allen (2009) claims that the clearest explanation for the UK location of the industrial revolution is seen by examining demand factors. By the eighteenth century cheap energy and high wages were both aspects of the British economy. As a result, the mechanisation of industry through inventions such as the steam engine and mechanical spinning was profitable because employers were able to save money on employees by spending on coal. At that time, Britain was the only country with significant deposits of coal.

a	
b	
c	

3 Techniques for paraphrasing

(a) Changing vocabulary by using synonyms:

argues > claims/ eighteenth century > 1700s/ wages > labour costs/ economise > saving

Do not attempt to paraphrase every word, since some have no true synonym e.g. demand, economy, energy

(b) Changing word class:

explanation (n.) > explain (v.) / mechanical (adj.) > mechanise (v.) / profitable (adj.) > profitability (n.)

(c) Changing word order:

. . . the best explanation for the British location of the industrial revolution is found by studying demand factors.

> A focus on demand may help explain the UK origin of the industrial revolution.

▶ See Units 3.2 Academic vocabulary and 3.11 Synonyms

4 Practice exercise: Paraphrasing

■ Read the following text and then practise the techniques illustrated above.

4.1   **FOUR WHEELS GOOD**

The growth of the car industry parallels the development of modern capitalism. It began in France and Germany, but took off in the United States. There Henry Ford adapted the moving production line from the Chicago meat industry to motor manufacturing, thus inventing mass production. In the 1920s Alfred Sloan's management theories helped General Motors to become the world's dominant car company. After the Second World War the car makers focused on the styling of their products, to encourage more frequent model changes.
From the 1970s there was criticism of the industry due to the inefficiency of most vehicles, which used petrol wastefully.
At the same time, trades unions became increasingly militant in defence of their members' jobs. Today the industry owns some of the most famous brands in the world. However, many car makers are currently threatened by increased competition and saturated markets.

---

5 Practice exercise: Synonyms

■ Find synonyms for the words underlined.

(a) The <u>growth</u> of the <u>car</u> industry <u>parallels</u> the <u>development</u> of <u>modern</u> capitalism.

   Example: The <u>rise</u> of the <u>automobile</u> industry <u>matches</u> the <u>progress</u> of <u>contemporary</u> capitalism.

(b) It <u>began</u> in France and Germany, but <u>took off</u> in the United States.

(c) There Henry Ford <u>adapted</u> the moving <u>production</u> line from the Chicago meat industry to <u>motor</u> manufacturing, <u>thus</u> inventing mass production.

6 Practice exercise: Word class

■ **Change the word class of the underlined words, and then rewrite the sentences.**

(a) In the 1920s Alfred Sloan's <u>management</u> theories <u>helped</u> General Motors to become the world's <u>dominant</u> car company.

> *Example*: In the 1920s, with help from the managerial theories of Alfred Sloan, General Motors dominated the world's car companies.

(b) After the Second World War the car makers <u>focused</u> on the <u>styling</u> of their products, to encourage more frequent model changes.

(c) From the 1970s there was <u>criticism</u> of the industry due to the <u>inefficiency</u> of most vehicles, which used petrol <u>wastefully</u>.

7 Practice exercise: Word order

■ **Change the word order of the following sentences (other changes may be needed).**

(a) At the same time, trades unions became increasingly militant in defence of their members' jobs.

> *Example*: At the same time increasingly militant trades unions defended their members' jobs.

(b) Today the industry owns some of the most famous brands in the world.

(c) However, many car makers are currently threatened by increased competition and saturated markets.

8 Practice exercise: Paraphrasing

■ Combine all these techniques to paraphrase the text 'Four wheels good' as fully as possible.

9 Practice exercise: Paraphrasing

■ Use the same techniques to paraphrase the following text.

9.1	GREEN DREAMS

It is often argued that governments can create employment and reduce carbon emissions by investing in renewable energy projects. These so-called 'green jobs' have the appeal of also helping to combat global warming while reducing a country's dependence on imported fuels. An American thinktank has calculated that the spending of $100 billion by the US government would result in the creation of two million jobs. A number of countries such as Germany, Spain and Indonesia have spent heavily on subsidising low-carbon technology.

However, critics of these schemes claim that the results are not as beneficial as they seem. Firstly, if the money was spent on other projects such as road building,

continued . . .

cont.   jobs would also be created. Secondly, higher government borrowing to
           pay for the investment has to be financed by the taxpayer, and it may
eventually affect the cost of borrowing for all businesses. In addition, subsidising
relatively inefficient energy sources such as solar and wind power will raise the
price of electricity for consumers.

A study in Spain looked at the cost of subsidising renewable energy over 25 years.
The estimated expenditure of €29 billion will provide 50,000 jobs, but they will
have cost €570,000 each to create. If, however, the government had allowed
private industry to spend the same amount, it would have created 113,000 posts;
more than twice as many. So it can be argued that the Spanish scheme will have
actually destroyed over 50,000 jobs.

Although these figures ignore both the environmental benefits and advantages for
Spain of reducing demand for imported fossil fuels, it is clear that such green
schemes do not automatically bring benefits to all.

Summarising

Making oral summaries is a common activity, for example when describing a film or a book. In academic writing it is a vital skill, allowing the writer to condense lengthy sources into a concise form. Like most skills it becomes easier with practice, and this unit explains the basic steps needed to achieve an accurate summary.

1 Summarising

■ **Write a summary of one of the topics below in no more than 20 words.**

(a) One of your parents

(b) A town or city you know well

(c) A product you have recently bought

■ Compare your summary with others in your group. What is needed for
a good summary?

•

_____

•

_____

•

_____

2 Stages of summarising

Summarising is a flexible tool. You can use it to give a one-sentence
synopsis of an article, or to provide much more detail, depending on your
writing needs. But in every case the same basic steps need to be followed
in order to meet the criteria listed above.

■ Study the stages of summary writing below and complete the gaps
with suitable words (one word per gap).

(a) Read the original text carefully and check any _____
vocabulary.

(b) _____ the key points by underlining or
highlighting.

(c) Make _____ of the key points, paraphrasing where
possible.

(d) Write the _____ from your notes, re-organising the
structure if needed.

(e) Check the summary to ensure it is _____ and
nothing important has been changed or lost.

3 Practice exercise: Summarising

■ Read the text (3.1) on the following page and the summaries (a)–(c).
Rate them 1 (best) to 3.

(a) Disruptive technology, according to two researchers from the
Harvard Business School, is a new invention which attracts
enough buyers to become established in the market, and then

> ### 3.1 DISRUPTIVE TECHNOLOGY
>
> This phrase was first used by Joseph Bower and Clayton Christensen, of the Harvard Business School, in 1995. They employed it to describe a new technology that appeals to a minority section of the market, but a large enough minority to allow the technology to take root and develop. Companies that continue to use the older technology run the risk of being left behind if they do not adopt the innovation at the right moment. A clear example in the mid-1990s was the digital camera. The first models had lower picture quality than film cameras and were expensive. But their important advantages were the ability of the photographer to see the results immediately, and being able to download the images to a computer for storage, printing or emailing. Since then, digital cameras have completely transformed the industry. The business of making film has almost vanished, and the vast majority of cameras sold are now digital.

to improve and grow. For example, the first digital cameras, launched in the mid-1990s, took poor quality pictures and were costly, but had some important benefits. Today they dominate the market, and the older type of camera which uses film is now a niche market.

(b) Bower and Christensen introduced the term 'disruptive technology' in 1995, to characterise a new technology which sold well enough to enter the market, and could then be developed further. The digital camera, for instance, was originally expensive and had low picture quality. However, its significant advantages of immediate results and producing images which could be processed on a computer, quickly allowed it to virtually replace traditional film cameras.

(c) Digital cameras are a good example of a disruptive technology, a term used by Bower and Christensen of Harvard Business School in 1995 to describe a new technology that initially wins enough market share to survive and develop. These cameras at first produced inferior pictures, but had the advantages of showing the photo instantly, and allowing the user to download the image. In a few years they became dominant in the camera market, while traditional film cameras were almost redundant.

4 Practice exercise: Summarising

■ Read the following text and underline the key points.

4.1 WEALTH AND FERTILITY

For most of the past century an inverse correlation between human fertility and economic development has been found. This means that as a country got richer, the average number of children born to each woman got smaller. While in the poorest countries women often have eight children, the rate fell as low as 1.3 in some European countries such as Italy, which is below the replacement rate. Such a low rate has two likely negative consequences: the population will fall in the long term, and a growing number of old people will have to be supported by a shrinking number of young. But a recent study by researchers from Pennsylvania University suggests that this pattern may be changing. They related countries' fertility rates to their human development index (HDI), a figure with a maximum value of 1.0, which assesses life expectancy, average income and education level. Over 20 countries now have an HDI of more than 0.9, and in a majority of these the fertility rate has started to increase, and in some is approaching two children per woman. Although there are exceptions such as Japan, it appears that ever higher levels of wealth and education eventually translate into a desire for more children.

▶ See Unit 1.5 Finding key points and note-making

5 Practice exercise: Summarising

■ Complete the notes of the key points below.

(a) Falling levels of fertility have generally been found

_____

_____

(b) In some, number of children born

_____

_____

(c) Two results: smaller populations and

_____

_____

(d) Recent research claims that

_____

_____

(e) Comparison of HDI (human development index:

_____

_____) with fertility found that in most highly rated (+0.9)

countries, _____

_____ .

6 Practice exercise: Summarising

■ **Join the notes together and expand them to make the final summary.
Check that the meaning is clear and no important points have been
left out.**

```



```

7 Practice exercise: Summarising

The summary in (6) is about 35 per cent of the original length, but it could be summarised further.

■ **Summarise the summary in no more than 20 words.**

8 Practice exercise: Summarising

■ **Summarise the following text in about 50 words.**

8.1 THE LAST WORD IN LAVATORIES?

Toto is a leading Japanese manufacturer of bathroom ceramic ware, with annual worldwide sales of around $5 bn. One of its best-selling ranges is the Washlet lavatory, priced at up to $5,000 and used in most Japanese homes. This has features such as a heated seat, and can play a range of sounds. This type of toilet is successful in its home market since many flats are small and crowded, and bathrooms provide valued privacy. Now Toto hopes to increase its sales in Europe and America, where it faces a variety of difficulties. European countries tend to have their own rules about lavatory design, so that different models have to be made for each market. Although Toto claims that its Washlet design uses less water than the average model, one factor which may impede its penetration into Europe is its need for an electrical socket for installation, as these are prohibited in bathrooms by most European building regulations.

References and quotations

Academic writing depends on the research and ideas of others, so it is vital to show which sources you have used in your work, in an acceptable manner. This unit explains the format of in-text citation, the use of quotations and the layout of reference sections.

1 Referring to sources

It is important to refer to the work of other writers that you have used. You may present these sources as either a summary/paraphrase or a quotation. In both cases a citation is included to provide a link to the list of references at the end of your paper.

■ Underline the citations in the following examples. Which is a summary and which a quotation? What are the advantages of each?

Friedman (1974) pointed out that inflation was effectively a kind of taxation.

As Friedman stated: 'Inflation is the one form of taxation that can be imposed without legislation' (1974: 93).

2 Practice exercise: References

There are three principal reasons for providing references:

(a) to show that you have read some of the authorities on the subject, which will give added weight to your writing;

(b) to allow the reader to find the source, if he/she wishes to examine the topic in more detail;

(c) to avoid plagiarism.

▶ **See Unit 1.3 Avoiding plagiarism**

■ **Decide if you need to give a reference in the following cases.**

	Citation Y/N
(a) Data you found from your own primary research	
(b) A graph from an internet article	
(c) A quotation from a book	
(d) An item of common knowledge	
(e) A theory from a journal article	
(f) An idea of your own based on reading several sources	

3 Reference verbs and systems

Summaries and quotations are usually introduced by a reference verb:

Friedman (1974) **pointed out** that . . .

▶ **See Unit 3.14 Verbs of reference**

These verbs can be either in the present or the past tense. Normally the use of the present tense suggests that the source is recent and still valid, while the past indicates that the source is older and may be out of date, but there are no hard-and-fast distinctions; Friedman's statement still has validity today.

There are several systems of referencing in use in the academic world, but most business schools use the Harvard system, which is explained here. You should ask your teachers if you are not sure which to use. With any system, the most important point is to be consistent.

4 Using quotations

Using a quotation means bringing the original words of a writer into your work. Quotations are effective in some situations, but must not be over-used. They can be valuable:

- when the original words express an idea in a distinctive way

- when the original is more concise than your summary could be

- when the original version is well-known (as in the quote from Friedman in §1, p. 58).

All quotations should be introduced by a phrase that shows the source, and also explains how this quotation fits into your argument:

Introductory phrase	Author	Reference verb	Quotation	Citation
This view is widely shared;	as Friedman	stated:	'Inflation is the one form of taxation that can be imposed without legislation'	(1974: 93).

(a) Short quotations (2–3 lines) are shown by single quotation marks. Quotations inside quotations (nested quotations) use double:

   As James remarked: 'Martin's concept of "internal space" requires close analysis.'

(b) Longer quotations are either indented (given a wider margin) or are printed in smaller type.

(c) Page numbers should be given after the date.

(d) Care must be taken to ensure that quotations are the exact words of the original. If it is necessary to delete some words which are irrelevant, use points . . . to show where the missing section was.

(e) It may be necessary to insert a word or phrase into the quotation to clarify a point. This can be done by using square brackets [ ]:

> '[this second category of] products is distinguished by its high brand recognition and resistance to switching strategies . . . .'

5 Examples

Study the following paragraph from an article called 'The Mobile Revolution' in the journal *Development Quarterly* (Issue 34 pages 85–97, 2009) by K. Hoffman.

5.1   According to recent estimates there are at least 4 billion mobile phones in the world, and the majority of these are owned by people in the developing world. Ownership in the developed world reached saturation level by 2007, so countries such as China, India and Brazil now account for most of the growth. In the poorest countries, with weak transport networks and unreliable postal services, access to telecommunications is a vital tool for starting or developing a business, since it provides access to wider markets. Studies have shown that when household incomes rise, more money is spent on mobile phones than any other item.

(a) **Summary**

Hoffman (2009) stresses the critical importance of mobile phones in the developing world in the growth of small businesses.

(b) **Quotation**

According to Hoffman, mobile phone ownership compensates for the weaknesses of infrastructure in the developing world: 'In the poorest countries, with weak transport networks and unreliable postal services, access to telecommunications is a vital tool for starting or developing a business, since it provides access to wider markets' (2009: 87).

(c) **Summary and quotation**

Hoffman points out that most of the growth in mobile phone ownership now takes place in the developing world, where it has become crucial for establishing a business: '. . . access to telecommunications is a vital tool for starting or developing a business, since it provides access to wider markets' (2009: 87).

■ **Read the next paragraph of the same article, also on P. 87 of the source.**

> 5.2   In such countries the effect of phone ownership on GDP growth is much stronger than in the developed world, because the ability to make calls is being offered for the first time, rather than as an alternative to existing landlines. As a result, mobile phone operators have emerged in Africa, India and other parts of Asia that are larger and more flexible than Western companies, and which have grown by catering for poorer customers, being therefore well-placed to expand downmarket. In addition Chinese phone makers have successfully challenged the established Western companies in terms of quality as well as innovation. A further trend is the provision of services via the mobile network which offer access to information about healthcare or agricultural advice.

■ **(a) Write a summary of the main point, including a citation.**

■ (b) Introduce a quotation to show the key point, referring to the
source.

■ (c) Combine (a) and (b), again acknowledging the source.

6 Abbreviations in citations

In-text citations use the following abbreviations, derived from Latin and
printed in italics:

et al.: used when three or more authors are given. The full list
of names is given in the reference list.

ibid.: taken from the same source (i.e. the same page) as the
previous citation.

op. cit.: taken from the same source as previously, but a
different page.

7 Organising the list of references

At the end of an essay or report there must be a list of all the sources cited in the writing.

Note that the list is organised alphabetically by the family name of the author. You should be clear about the difference between first names and family names. On title pages the normal format of first name then family name is used:

Sheila Burford, Juan Gonzalez

But in citations only the family name is usually used:

Burford (2001), Gonzalez (1997)

In reference lists use the family name and the first initial:

Burford S., Gonzalez J.

If you are not sure which name is the family name, ask a classmate from that cultural background.

■ **Study the reference list on the following page and answer these questions.**

(a) Find an example of:

    (i)   a book by one author

    (ii)   a journal article

    (iii) a chapter in an edited book

    (iv) an article from a newspaper website

    (v)   an anonymous magazine article (electronic)

    (vi) an official report

(b) What are the main differences in the way these sources are referenced?

    (i)   _____

    (ii)   _____

    (iii) _____

7.1   **REFERENCES**

Brander, J. and Spencer, B. (1985) 'Export Subsidies and International Market Share Rivalry'. *Journal of International Economics* 18, 83–100

Cable, V. (1983) *Protectionism and Industrial Decline*. London: Hodder and Stoughton

Conrad, K. (1989) 'Productivity and Cost Gaps in Manufacturing Industries in US, Japan and Germany'. *European Economic Review* 33, 1135–1159

Gribben, R. (2009) 'Ministers Accelerate Support for Car Industry'. *The Daily Telegraph* online. Downloaded from: www.telegraph.co.uk/finance/newsbysector/transport/4975676/Ministers-accelerate-support-for-car-industry.html [12 March 2009]

Intriligator, M. (2005) 'Globalisation of the World Economy: Potential Benefits and Costs and a Net Assessment' in Gangopadhyay, R. and Chatterji, M. (eds) *Economics of Globalisation*. Aldershot: Ashgate 67–76

OECD (1998) *Open markets Matter. The Benefits of Trade and Investment Liberalisation*. Paris: OECD

The Economist (2009) 'Underpowered'. 16 April. Downloaded from: www.economist.com/world/britain/displaystory.cfm?story_id=13497452 [29 April 2009]

(iv) _____

(v) _____

(vi) _____

(c) When are italics used?

(d) How are capital letters used in titles?

(e) How is a source with no given author listed?

(f) Write citations for summaries from each of the sources.

(i) _____

(ii) _____

(iii) _____

(iv) _____

(v) _____

(vi) _____

(vii) _____

▶ For a full guide to the use of the Harvard system see: http://home.ched.coventry.ac.uk/caw/harvard/.

Combining sources

Most assignments expect students to read a variety of sources, often reflecting conflicting views on a topic. In some cases the contrast between the various views may be the focus of the task. This unit explains how a writer can present and organise a range of contrasting sources.

1 Mentioning sources

In the early stages of an essay it is common to discuss the contributions of other writers to the subject.

■ **Read the following example from a comparison of 'technology readiness' in Chinese and American consumers, and answer the questions below.**

1.1   The extent to which consumers desire to use new technology is commonly influenced by factors such as consumer attitudes toward specific technologies (Bobbit and Dabholkar, 2001; Curran *et al.*, 2003), the level of technology anxiety exhibited by consumers (Meuter, Ostrom, Bitner and Roundtree, 2003), and consumer capacity and willingness (Walker, Lees, Hecker and Francis, 2002). Mick and Fournier (1998) argue that consumers can simultaneously exhibit positive feelings (such as intelligence and efficacy) and negative feelings (such as ignorance and ineptitude) towards new technology. Venkatesh (2000) found that 'computer playfulness' and 'computer anxiety' serve as anchors that users employ in forming perceptions of ease of use about new technology.

(a) How many sources are mentioned here?

(b) What was the subject of Meuter, Ostrom, Bitner and Roundtree's research?

(c) Which source contrasted fear of computers with playing with computers?

(d) Which source examined the paradox of positive and negative attitudes to computers?

(e) How many sources are cited that studied attitudes to particular technologies?

2 Practice exercise: Sources

■ The two texts below (2.1a and b) reflect different approaches to the topic of globalisation. Read them both and then study the extract from an introduction to an essay that mentions the two sources. Answer the questions that follow.

2.1a   GLOBALISATION

It has been argued that globalisation is not a new phenomenon, but has its roots in the age of colonial development in the seventeenth and eighteenth centuries. However, its modern use can be dated to 1983, when Levitt's article 'The Globalisation of Markets' was published. Among the many definitions of the process that have been suggested, perhaps the simplest is that globalisation is the relatively free movement of services, goods, people and ideas worldwide. An indication of the positive effect of the process is that cross-border world trade, as a percentage of global GDP, was 15 per cent in 1990 but is expected to reach 30 per cent by 2015. Among the forces driving globalisation in the last two decades have been market liberalisation, cheap communication via the internet and telephony, and the growth of the BRIC (Brazil, Russia, India and China) economies.

Source: Costa, L. 2008

2.1b   **GLOBALISATION**

Considerable hostility to the forces of globalisation has been demonstrated in both
the developed and developing worlds. In the former, there is anxiety about the
outsourcing of manufacturing and service jobs to countries which offer cheaper
labour, while developing countries claim that only a minority have benefited from
the increase in world trade. They point out that per-capita income in the 20 poorest
countries has hardly changed in the past 40 years, while in the richest 20 it has
tripled. The markets of Western nations are still closed to agricultural products
from developing countries, and while there is free movement of goods and capital,
migration from poor countries to rich ones is tightly controlled.

Source: Lin, Y. 2006

2.2   **ESSAY EXTRACT**

Costa (2008) argues that globalisation, although not a modern phenomenon, has
recently accelerated, encouraged by forces such as the liberalisation of markets
and cheap communication. In particular it has had a powerful effect in increasing
world trade, especially benefiting the BRIC economies such as Brazil and China.
However, Lin (2006) emphasises the negative reactions that have been produced
by the process. She highlights the fears of unemployment in richer nations created
by outsourcing work, matched by the concerns of poorer states that they are not
sharing in the economic growth due to barriers to their trade and labour.

(a) The extract (2.2) summarises ideas from both Costa and Lin.
    Find an example of a summary in the extract (2.2) and match it
    with the original text in 2.1a or b.

Summary	Original

(b) Which verbs are used to introduce the summaries?

(c) Which word marks the point where the writer switches from considering Costa to dealing with Lin?

(d) What other words or phrases could be used at this point?

3 Practice exercise: Combining sources

■ Read the third text on globalisation below, and then complete the paragraph from an essay titled: 'Globalisation mainly benefits multi-national companies rather than ordinary people – Discuss', using all three sources.

3.1   Multi-national companies have undoubtedly benefited from the relaxation of the import tariff regimes which previously protected local firms, allowing them to operate more freely in markets such as India which have recently liberalised. These corporations have evolved two distinct approaches to the challenge of globalisation. Some, e.g. Gillette, have continued to produce their products in a few large plants with strict control to ensure uniform quality, while others, for instance Coca-Cola, vary the product to suit local tastes and tend to manufacture their goods on the spot. They claim that an understanding of regional differences is essential for competing with national rivals.

Source: Brokaw, P. 2002

Lin (2006) demonstrates

Organising paragraphs

Paragraphs are the basic building blocks of academic writing. Well-structured paragraphs help the reader understand the topic more easily by dividing up the argument into convenient sections. This unit looks at the components of paragraphs, the way the components are linked together, and also the linkage between paragraphs in the overall text.

1 Do paragraphs have a pattern?

■ Discuss the following questions.

- What is a paragraph?
- What is the normal length of a paragraph?
- Is there a standard structure for paragraphs?
- How is a paragraph linked together?

■ Study the example below.

1.1   SHOULD HOME OWNERSHIP BE ENCOURAGED?

The rate of home ownership varies widely across the developed world. Germany, for instance, has one of the lowest rates, at 42 per cent, while in Spain it is twice as high, 85 per cent. Both the USA and Britain have similar rates of about 69 per cent. The reasons for this variation appear to be more cultural and historic than economic, since high rates are found in both rich and poorer countries. There appears to be no conclusive link between national prosperity and the number of home owners.

The paragraph can be analysed:

1 Topic sentence	The rate of home ownership varies widely across the developed world.
2 Example 1	Germany, **for instance**, has one of the lowest rates, at 42%, **while** in Spain it is twice as high, 85%.
3 Example 2	Both the USA and Britain have similar rates of about 69%.
4 Reason	**The reasons for** this variation appear to be more cultural and historic than economic, **since** high rates are found in both rich and poorer countries.
5 Summary	**There appears to be** no conclusive link between national prosperity and numbers of home owners.

(a) A paragraph is a group of sentences which deal with a single topic.

(b) The length of paragraphs varies significantly according to text type, but should be no less than four or five sentences.

(c) Normally (but not always) the first sentence introduces the topic. Other sentences may give definitions, examples, information, reasons, restatements and summaries.

(d) The parts of the paragraph are linked together by the phrases and conjunctions shown in bold in the table. They guide the reader through the arguments presented.

2 Practice exercise: Paragraphs

■ **Read the next paragraph from the same essay and answer the questions below.**

> **2.1**   Despite this, many countries encourage the growth of home ownership. Ireland and Spain, for example, allow mortgage payers to offset payments against income tax. It is widely believed that owning your own home has social as well as economic benefits. Compared to renters, home owners are thought to be more stable members of the community who contribute more to local affairs. In addition, neighbourhoods of owner occupiers are considered to have less crime and better schools. But above all, ownership encourages saving and allows families to build wealth.

	Despite this, many countries encourage the growth of home ownership.
	Ireland and Spain, for example, allow mortgage payers to offset payments against income tax.
	It is widely believed that owning your own home has social as well as economic benefits.
	Compared to renters, home owners are thought to be more stable members of the community who contribute more to local affairs.
	In addition, neighbourhoods of owner occupiers are considered to have less crime and better schools.
	But above all, ownership encourages saving and allows families to build wealth.

(a) Analyse the paragraph by completing the left hand column in the table above with the following types of sentence:
Supporting point 1, Supporting point 2, Supporting point 3,
Example, Main reason, Topic.

(b) Underline the words and phrases used to link the sentences together.

(c) Which phrase is used to link this paragraph to the one before?

3 Development of ideas

■ **The sentences below form the third paragraph of the same essay, but they have been mixed up.**

(a) Use the table below to put them in the correct order.

(i)   When this burst, millions of people lost their homes, which for many had contained their savings.

(ii)   These had been developed to allow higher-risk poorer families to buy their own homes, but contributed to a property price bubble.

(iii) Many economists now argue that there is a maximum level of home ownership which should not be exceeded.

(iv)   All these claims were challenged by the economic crash of 2008, which was in large part caused by defaults on American sub-prime mortgages.

(v)   Even households which had positive equity still felt poorer and reduced their spending.

(vi)   Others were trapped in their houses by negative equity, in other words their houses were worth less than they had paid for them.

Topic sentence	
Definition	
Result 1	
Result 2	
Result 3	
Conclusion	

(b) Underline the phrase used to link the paragraph to the previous one.

(c) Underline the words and phrases used to link the paragraph together.

4 Linking paragraphs together

In the examples above, each new paragraph begins with a phrase that links it to the previous paragraph, in order to maintain continuity of argument:

> *Despite this* (i.e. the lack of a conclusive link)

> *All these claims* (i.e. arguments in favour of home ownership)

In order to begin a new topic you may use:

> *Turning to the issue of . . .*

> *Inflation must also be examined . . .*

> *. . . . . is another issue . . .*

Paragraphs can also be introduced with adverbs:

> *Traditionally, few examples were . . .*

> *Finally, the performance of . . .*

5 Practice exercise: Organising paragraphs

■ (a) Use the notes below to complete a paragraph of an essay titled: 'High rates of home ownership are bad for the economy – Discuss'.

- It is claimed that increases in rate of home ownership lead to unemployment

- Home ownership appears to make people more reluctant to move to find work

- E.g. Spain (high ownership + high unemployment) vs. Switzerland (low ownership + low unemployment)

- Theory still controversial – other factors have been proposed

- E.g. liquidity of housing markets (how easy to sell houses)

1	It has been argued that rises in the rate of home ownership can increase the rate of unemployment.
2	
3	
4	
5	

■ **(b) Use the notes below to write the next paragraph of the essay, including a phrase linking it to the previous paragraph.**

- Recession of 2008–9 gave support to theory in US states (e.g. California, Michigan and Florida)

- They had major housing boom in 1990s

- After recession rate of house moving fell sharply

- One factor was number of households in negative equity

- Having negative equity means selling house at loss

- High rates of ownership may deepen recession if labour is more static

1	
2	

3	
4	
5	
6	

Introductions and conclusions

Any piece of writing needs an effective introduction to tell the reader what to expect, which should also encourage further reading. The conclusion should provide a clear answer to any question asked in the title, as well as summarising the main points. In coursework both introductions and conclusions are normally written after the main body.

1 Introduction contents

Introductions are usually no more than about 10 per cent of the total length of the assignment. Therefore in a 2,000-word essay the introduction would be about 200 words.

■ **(a) What would commonly be found in an introduction? Add your ideas to the list below.**

- *a definition of any difficult words in the title*
- _____
- _____
- _____
- _____
- _____
- _____

■ **(b) Read the extracts below from introductions to articles and decide which of the functions listed above they illustrate.**

(i)   The goal of the present study is to complement the existing body of knowledge on HR practices with a large-scale empirical study, and at the same time contribute to the discussion on why some firms are more innovative than others.

(ii)   We consider three dimensions of customer satisfaction: service, quality and price. We argue that employees most directly influence customer satisfaction with service . . . . We test this proposition empirically, and then examine the links between customer satisfaction and sales.

(iii)   Corporate governance is a set of mechanisms, both institutional and market-based, designed to mitigate agency problems that arise from the separation of ownership and control in a company, protect the interests of all stakeholders, improve from performance and ensure that investors get an adequate return on their investment.

(iv)   This study will focus on mergers in the media business between 1990 and 2005, since with more recent examples an accurate assessment of the consequences cannot yet be made.

(v)   The rest of the paper is organised as follows. The second section explains why corporate governance is important for economic prosperity. The third section presents the model specification and describes the data and variables used in our empirical analysis. The fourth section reports and discusses the empirical results. The fifth section concludes.

(vi)   The use of incentive compensation, such as bonus and stock options, is an important means of motivating and compensating executives of private companies, especially executives of technology-orientated companies.

(vii)   There is no clear empirical evidence sustaining a 'managerial myopia' argument. Pugh *et al.* (1992) find evidence that supports such theory, but Meulbrook *et al.* (1990), Mahoney *et al.* (1997), Garvey and Hanka (1999) and a study by the Office of the Chief Economist of the Securities and Exchange Commission (1985) find no evidence.

2 Introduction structure

Not every introduction will include all the elements listed above.

■ Which are essential and which are optional?

There is no standard pattern for an introduction, since much depends on the type of research you are conducting and the length of your work, but a common framework is:

a	Definition of key terms, if needed
b	Relevant background information
c	Review of work by other writers on the topic
d	Purpose or aim of the paper
e	Your methods and the results you found
f	Any limitations you imposed
g	The organisation of your work

(a) Certain words or phrases in the title may need clarifying because they are not widely understood.

> For the purpose of this paper I define serendipity as search leading to unintended discovery.

▶ See Unit 2.5 Definitions

(b) It is useful to remind the reader of the wider context of your work. This may also show the importance and value of the study you have carried out.

> A major strength of this study is the theoretically-informed context-embedded selection of HR practices in explaining why some firms are more innovative than others.

(c) While a longer article may have a separate literature review, in a shorter essay it is still important to show familiarity with researchers who have studied this topic previously.

The last few years have, indeed, witnessed many notable
interventions and seminal articulations of the pros and
cons of globalisation for perceived disadvantaged groups,
including workers (Haq, 2003; Horgan, 2001; Klein, 2000;
Rai, 2001) . . .

(d) The aim of your research must be clearly stated so the reader is clear
what you are trying to do.

The key question addressed in this study is a simple one:
Is innovativeness a link between pay and performance
in the technology sector?

(e) The method demonstrates the process that you undertook to achieve
the aim given before.

Using a sample of 988 Dutch firms, the relationship between
a set of six HR practices and the fraction of radically and
incrementally changed products in a firm's total sales is
explored.

(f) Clearly you cannot deal with every aspect of this topic in an essay,
so you must make clear the boundaries of your study.

The focus will be on corporate governance in South Asian
companies . . .

(g) Understanding the structure of your work will help the reader to
follow your argument.

The paper deals with these points as follows. The first section
describes the concept of serendipity and offers a framework
that integrates serendipity within the entrepreneurship
literature. The following section discusses . . .

3 Opening sentences

It can be difficult to start writing an essay, but especially in exams, hesitation
will waste valuable time. The first few sentences should be general but not
vague, to help the reader focus on the topic. They often have the following
pattern:

Time phrase	Topic	Development
Currently,	marketing theory	is being re-assessed.
Since 2005	electric vehicles	have become a serious commercial proposition.

It is important to avoid opening sentences that are over-general. Compare:

> Nowadays there is a lot of competition among different providers of news.

> Newspapers are currently facing strong competition from rival news providers such as the internet and television.

■ **Write introductory sentences for three of the following titles.**

(a) How important is it for companies to have women as senior managers?

(b) What are the 'pull' factors in international tourism?

(c) What is the relationship between inflation and unemployment?

(d) 'Monopolies are inefficient in using resources' – Discuss.

▶ **See Unit 2.7 Generalisations**

4 Practice exercise: Introductions

You have to write an essay titled 'State control of industry: does it have any benefits?'

■ **Using the notes below and your own ideas, write a short introduction for the essay (it is not necessary to refer to sources in this exercise).**

Definition – State control = public ownership, especially of 'natural monopoly' industries, e.g. electricity, water supply.

Background – world wide trend to privatise industries but subject to controversy, e.g. postal service, railways.

Aim – to establish what advantages may come from public ownership of these industries.

Method – Compare advantages (security of supply, benefits of large-scale operation) and disadvantages (lack of competition, corruption, political control) in UK and France, in two industries: railways and electricity.

Limitation – from 1990–2005

5 Conclusions

Conclusions tend to be shorter and more diverse than introductions. Some articles may have a 'summary' or 'concluding remarks'. But student papers should generally have a final section, which summarises the arguments and makes it clear to the reader that the original question has been answered.

■ **Which of the following are generally acceptable in conclusions?**

(a) A statement showing how your aim has been achieved.

(b) A discussion of the implications of your research.

(c) Some new information on the topic not mentioned before.

(d) A short review of the main points of your study.

(e) Some suggestions for further research.

(f) The limitations of your study.

(g) Comparison with the results of similar studies.

(h) A quotation which appears to sum up your work.

■ **Match the extracts from conclusions below with the acceptable components above.**

Example: a = vi

(i) As always, this investigation has a number of limitations to be considered in evaluating its findings.

(ii) Obviously, business expatriates could benefit from being informed that problem-focused coping strategies are more effective than symptom-focused ones.

(iii) Another line of research worth pursuing further is to study the importance of language for expatriate assignments.

(iv) Our review of 13 studies of strikes in public transport demonstrates that the effect of a strike on public transport ridership varies and may either be temporary or permanent . . .

(v) These results of the Colombia study reported here are consistent with other similar studies conducted in other countries (Baron and Norman, 1992).

(vi) This study has clearly illustrated the drawbacks to family ownership of retail businesses.

6 Practice exercise: Conclusions

■ Look at Unit 1.10 Organising paragraphs, section 5. Study the notes for the first two paragraphs, then write a concluding paragraph that summarises the main points and answers the question in the title (i.e. Are high rates of home ownership bad for the economy?). Discuss any implications that arise and suggest possible further research.

Rewriting and proof-reading

In exams you have no time for rewriting, but for coursework assignments it is important to take time to revise your work to improve its clarity and logical development. In both situations proof-reading is essential to avoid the small errors that may make your work inaccurate or even incomprehensible.

1 Rewriting

Although it is tempting to think that the first draft of an essay is adequate, it is almost certain that it can be improved. After completing your first draft you should leave it for a day and then re-read it, asking the following questions.

(a) Does this fully answer the question(s) in the title?

(b) Do the different sections of the paper have the right weight, i.e. is it well balanced?

(c) Does the argument or discussion develop clearly and logically?

(d) Have I forgotten any important points which would support the development?

2 Practice exercise: Rewriting

You have written the first draft of a 2,000-word essay titled: 'Assess the relevance of motivation theories for today's managers in assisting them to increase employee performance, using the case of a Japanese car producer operating in the UK.'

■ **Study the introduction to this essay below, and decide how it could be improved, by listing your suggestions in the table.**

> **2.1** In the modern commercial society of today, the success of companies does not just rely on the external business environment, but more importantly depends on the internal management of human resources, due to the inseparable relationship between employee performance and the achievement of companies. Thus, the employees play a significant role in the development of companies, and their performance is determined by ability, work environment and motivation. Nowadays, organisations pay increasing attention to the importance of motivating employees. This essay will present a clear theoretical framework of work motivation, and then concentrate on evaluating the empirical relevance of those theories.

(a)	*Rather short (100 words) for an introduction to a 2,000-word essay*
(b)	
(c)	
(d)	
(e)	

With these points in mind, the introduction could be rewritten as follows:

> In the current commercial environment, the success of companies does not just rely on the external business climate, but more importantly depends on the internal management of human resources, due to the inseparable relationship between employee performance and the achievement of companies (Agarwala, 2003). Thus, the employees play a significant role in the development of companies, and their performance is determined by ability, work environment and motivation (Griffin, 1990).
>
> Consequently, employee motivation is an increasingly important concern for companies. This essay will first present a clear theoretical framework of work motivation, focusing on Maslow's hierarchy of needs theory and Herzberg's two-factor theory. The second section will concentrate on evaluating the empirical relevance of those theories, by analysing the measures taken by the Japanese car producer Toyota to motivate its British employees.

3 Practice exercise: Rewriting

■ Read the draft conclusion to the same essay and decide how it could be improved. Rewrite the conclusion.

3.1   To conclude, it has been shown that the hierarchy of needs theory of Maslow, Herzberg's two-factor theory and the achievement theory of McClelland have some relevance to the motivation of British employees. The application of these theories has sometimes resulted in increased employee performance. Some limitations to the application of these theories have been demonstrated. Cross-cultural problems have arisen. Knowledge workers need different motivation methods. The older theories of motivation are not always relevant to today's workplace. This kind of organisational experience needs a more up-to-date theoretical basis.

4 Proof-reading

(a) Proof-reading means checking your work for small errors which may make it more difficult for the reader to understand exactly what you want to say. If a sentence has only one error:

> **She has no enough interpersonal skills to handle different relationships . . .**

it is not difficult to understand, but if there are multiple errors, even though they are all quite minor, the cumulative effect is very confusing:

> **Demolition of sevral uk banks like northren Rock and may others . . .**

Clearly, you should aim to make your meaning as clear as possible. Note that computer spellchecks do not always help you, since they may ignore a word that is spelt correctly but that is not the word you meant to use:

> **Tow factors need to be considered . . .**

■ (b) Examples of the most common types of error in student writing are shown below. In each case underline the error and correct it.

(i)   **factual:** corruption is a problem in many countries such as Africa

(ii)   **word ending:** she was young and innocence

(iii) **punctuation:** some manufacturers for instance Toyota have begun . . .

(iv)   **tense:** until the early 1980s, there were about 15 assemblers that produce vehicles . . .

(v)   **vocabulary:** . . . vital to the successfulness of a company operating in China

(vi)   **spelling:** pervious experience can sometimes give researchers . . .

(vii) **singular/plural:** the value concept play a crucial role . . .

(viii) **style:** . . . finally, the essay will conclude with a conclusion

(ix)   **missing word:** an idea established by David Ricardo in nineteenth century

(x)   **word order:** a rule of marketing which states that consumers when go out shopping . . .

■ (c) The following extracts each contain one type of error. Match each to one of the examples i–x above, and correct the error.

(i)   Products like Tiger biscuits are well-known to kids . . .

(ii)   Both companies focus on mass marketing to promote its line of products.

(iii) Failure to find the right product may lead to torment for consumers.

(iv)   . . . different researchers have differently effects on the research.

(v)   After the single European market was established in 1873 . . .

(vi)   . . . experienced researchers can most likely come over these problems.

(vii)   Firstly because, it provides them with an opportunity of borrowing capital . . .

(viii) The company selected Hungry for setting up its development centre.

(ix)   These cases demonstrate why companies from the rest of world are eager to . . .

(x)   Since 2003, few companies entered the French market . . .

■ **(d) Underline the errors in the paragraph below and then rewrite it.**

4.1   OPPORTUNITIES FOR NON-EUROPEAN BUSINESSES IN EUROPE

Many non-European businesses are aiming to enter single European market as they see an unexploited potential there. There are three reasons of this interest. Firstly the non-european organisations are keen to do a business in the European markets because it is one of leading investment destination and easiest place to set up and run a business. Secondly, the single European market provide forein investors with an internationally competitive tax environment.

---

5 Confusing pairs

When proofreading, it is important to check for mistakes with some confusing pairs of words, which can have similar but distinct spellings and meanings, e.g.

The drought **affected** the wheat harvest in Australia

An immediate **effect** of the price rise was a fall in demand

'Affect' and 'effect' are two different words. 'Affect' is a verb, while 'effect' is commonly used as a noun.

■ Study the differences between other similar confusing pairs (most
common use in brackets).

---

accept (verb)/except (prep)

It is difficult to **accept** their findings

The report is finished **except** for the conclusion

---

compliment (noun/verb)/complement (verb)

Her colleagues **complimented** her on her presentation

His latest book **complements** his previous research on third world debt

---

economic (adj)/economical (adj)

Sharing a car to work was an **economical** move

Inflation was one **economic** result of the war

---

its (pronoun)/it's (pronoun + verb)

It's widely agreed that carbon emissions are rising

The car's advanced design was **its** most distinct feature

---

lose (verb)/loose (adj)

No general ever plans to **lose** a battle

He stressed the **loose** connection between religion and psychology

---

principal (adj/noun)/principle (noun)

All economists recognise the **principle** of supply and demand

Zurich is the **principal** city of Switzerland

---

rise (verb – past tense rose)/raise (verb – past tense raised)

The population of London **rose** by 35 per cent in the century

The university **raised** its fees by 10 per cent last year

---

site (noun)/sight (noun)

The **site** of the battle is now covered by an airport

His **sight** began to weaken when he was in his eighties

---

tend to (verb)/trend (noun)

Young children **tend** to enjoy making a noise

In many countries there is a **trend** towards smaller families

■ **Choose the correct word in each sentence.**

(a) The company was founded on the <u>principals/principles</u> of quality and value.

(b) Millions of people are attempting to <u>lose/loose</u> weight.

(c) Sunspots have been known to <u>affect/effect</u> radio communication.

(d) Professor Poledna received their <u>compliments/complements</u> politely.

(e) The ancient symbol depicted a snake eating <u>it's/its</u> tail.

(f) Both social and <u>economical/economic</u> criteria need to be examined.

(g) It took many years for some of Keynes' theories to be <u>accepted/excepted</u>.

Elements of writing

Argument and discussion

On most courses it is not enough to show that you are familiar with the leading authorities. Students are expected to study the conflicting views on any topic and engage with them. This means analysing and critiquing them if appropriate. This unit presents ways of demonstrating your familiarity with both sides of the argument and giving your own views in a suitably academic manner.

1 Discussion vocabulary

Essay titles commonly ask students to 'discuss' a topic:

> 'Discuss the potential benefits of countertrade to a multinational company.'

This requires an evaluation of both the benefits and disadvantages of the topic, with a section of the essay, sometimes headed 'Discussion', in which a summary of these is made. The following vocabulary can be used:

+	−
benefit	drawback
advantage	disadvantage
a positive aspect	a negative feature
pro (informal)	con (informal)
plus (informal)	minus (informal)
one major advantage is . . .	a serious drawback is . . .

2 Organisation

The discussion section can be organised in two ways; either by grouping the benefits and disadvantages together, or by examining the subject from different viewpoints. For example, the following essay title can be discussed in the two ways as shown:

> 'Environmental considerations have no place in a company's strategy – Discuss.'

(a) grouping all the drawbacks together in one or more paragraphs, then treating the benefits in the same way:

Drawbacks: May increase costs (e.g. 'green' electricity)/delay projects/extra work for managers
Benefits: May save money (e.g. reduced packaging)/good PR = increased sales/employee job satisfaction may also be increased
Discussion: Depends on nature of business/some costs will rise, others fall/important long-term benefits as consumers place more weight on 'green' considerations

(b) examining the subject from different viewpoints, e.g. economic, ethical or social:

Economic: Initial investment in energy-saving measures may increase costs but long-term benefits should follow
Ethical: Responsible companies should play a part in combating climate change
Social: Consumer-facing companies benefit from 'green' credentials = increased sales/employee job satisfaction may also be increased
Discussion: Depends on nature of business/some costs will rise, others fall/important long-term benefits as consumers place more weight on 'green' considerations

3 Practice exercise: Argument and discussion

You have to write an essay titled:

'Discuss whether some employees should be permitted to work from home.'

■ **Brainstorm the positive and negative aspects in the box below, and then write an outline using one of the structures (a) or (b) above.**

+	−

Discuss whether some employees should be permitted to work from home

Outline

(a)

(b)

(c)

(d)

---

4 Language of discussion

Avoid personal phrases such as *in my opinion* or *personally, I think* . . .

Use impersonal phrases instead, such as:

It is generally accepted that	working from home saves commuting time . . .
It is widely agreed that	email and the internet reduce reliance on an office . . .
Most people appear	to need face-to-face contact with colleagues . . .
It is probable that	more companies will encourage working from home . . .
The evidence suggests that	certain people are better at self-management . . .

Certain phrases suggest a minority viewpoint:

It can be argued that	home-working encourages time-wasting
Some people believe that	home-workers become isolated

5 Counter-arguments

In a discussion you must show that you are familiar with both sides of the argument, and provide reasons to support your position. It is usual to deal with the counter-arguments first, before giving your view.

■ **Study the example below, and write two more sentences using ideas from the title in Section 3.**

Counter-argument	Your position
Some people believe that home-workers become isolated,	*but this can be avoided by holding weekly meetings for all departmental staff.*

6 Providing evidence

Useful discussion is based on evidence that you have studied the relevant sources on a topic. Only then can you give a balanced judgement.

■ **First study the paragraph on the next page, which discusses the value of imports to an economy.**

After you have studied the paragraph on the next page, complete the diagram below of the paragraph's structure using the following descriptors:

Writer's viewpoint

Benefits of imports – Indian case study (Goldberg *et al.*)

Drawbacks of imports – Inglehart

1	
2	
3	

6.1 THE IMPORTANCE OF IMPORTS

It has frequently been argued that economies benefit from exports, while imports are a regrettable necessity. According to Inglehart (1994), for instance, import controls play an essential role in preventing the unsupportable growth of trade deficits. Governments regularly support export-orientated industries in the belief that their success can strengthen the economy. However, a different view is put forward by Goldberg *et al.* (2009). Their study of the experience of India after it was forced to reduce import tariffs by the IMF in 1991 demonstrates that this led to substantial economic benefits. By permitting capital goods to be imported more cheaply, existing production could be achieved at lower cost, while there was also a growth in the range of new products. Overall, manufacturing output increased by 25 per cent in the six years after 1991. It appears that the traditional economic bias against imports may well be unfounded.

7 Practice exercise: Argument and discussion

■ Write a paragraph on the topic:

'Inflation can be a positive force in the economy – Discuss.'

■ Use the ideas below and give your viewpoint.

Pros: Encourages spending as people expect higher prices in future
Reduces the value of debt
The opposite, deflation, causes stagnation
Source: Costa *et al.*, 2000

Cons: Workers demand large pay rises, leads to conflict
Excessive inflation leads to loss of faith in money
Creates uncertainty about future
Source: Patterson, 1998

Cause and effect

Academic work frequently involves demonstrating a link between a cause, such as a price rise, and an effect, such as a fall in demand. This unit explains two methods of describing the link, with the focus either on the cause or on the effect.

1 The language of cause and effect

A writer may choose to put the emphasis on either the cause or the effect. In both cases, either a verb or a conjunction can be used to show the link.

(a) Focus on causes

With verbs		
The recession	caused created led to resulted in produced	high unemployment
With conjunctions		
Because of Due to Owing to As a result of	**the recession**	there was high unemployment

(b) Focus on effects

With verbs		
High unemployment	was caused by was produced by resulted from (note use of passives)	the recession
With conjunctions		
There was **high unemployment**	due to because of as a result of	the recession

■ **Compare the following:**

Because prices **were** cut sales rose   (because + verb)

Because of the **price cuts** sales rose   (because of + noun)

As/Since prices **were** cut sales rose   (conjunction + verb)

Owing to/Due to the **price cuts** sales rose   (conjunction + noun)

Conjunctions are commonly used with specific situations, while verbs are more often used in general cases:

Printing money commonly **leads to** inflation (general)

Due to July's hot weather demand for ice cream increased (specific)

2 Practice exercise: Cause and effect

■ Match the causes with their likely effects and write sentences linking them together.

Cold winter of 1995	increase in labour disputes
Tax cuts	redundancies
Introduction of digital cameras	higher levels of spending
Increase in interest rates last spring	higher levels of saving
Falling sales of a firm's products	**increased demand for electricity**
His aggressive managerial style	reduced demand for photographic film

(a) _____

_____

(b) _____

_____

(c) _____

_____

(d) _____

_____

(e) _____

_____

(f) _____

_____

3 Practice exercise: Cause and effect

■ Complete the following sentences with likely effects.

(a) Increasing use of the internet for shopping

_____

(b) Rising demand for MBA courses

_____

(c) Lower fuel prices

_____

(d) Bad weather in the Brazilian coffee-producing region

_____

■ **Complete these sentences with possible causes.**

(e) The company's bankruptcy

_____

(f) The drop in share prices

_____

(g) Hiring extra staff

_____

(h) A significant rise in profits

_____

4 Practice exercise: Cause and effect

■ **Use conjunctions or verbs to complete the following paragraph.**

4.1 UNHAPPY WORKERS

In recent years there appears to have been a growth in employee dissatisfaction
with work. At its most extreme this is shown by high rates of suicide in some
companies, apparently (a) _____ the stress (b) _____
_____ re-structuring programmes. Surveys of both European and American
employees have found that more than 50 per cent were unhappy, often (c)
_____ a feeling of stagnation. Various theories have attempted
to explain this situation. Employees in certain industries such as car production
may feel stressed (d) _____ industry-wide

---

continued . . .

| cont. | overcapacity, creating a sense of insecurity. More generally, recession |

can (e) _____ fear of unemployment or short-time

working. In addition, the constant drive to cut costs and increase productivity

(f) _____ a concern with meeting targets which takes its toll on

the workforce. Furthermore, many younger employees are now hired on short-

term contracts, which (g) _____ an awareness that they could lose

their jobs with little warning.

5 Practice exercise: Cause and effect

■ Study the flow chart below, which shows some of the possible effects of a higher oil price. Complete the paragraph describing this sequence.

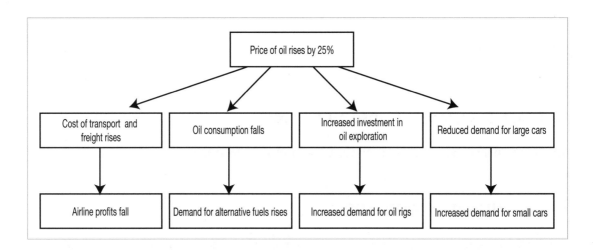

An increase of 25 per cent in the price of oil would have numerous results. Firstly, it would lead to ...

6 Practice exercise: Cause and effect

■ Choose one of the following situations. Draw a flow chart showing some probable effects, and write a paragraph to describe them.

(a) A property price bubble.

(b) Interest rates reduced below 1 per cent by the central bank.

Cohesion

Cohesion means joining a text together with reference words
(e.g. he, theirs, the former) and linkers or conjunctions so that
the whole text is clear and readable. This unit practises the use of
reference words, while linkers are examined in Unit 3.5.

1 Reference language

Reference words are used to avoid repetition:

MAZ is a Turkish engineering company with **its** head office in
Ankara. **It** is divided into **five divisions** and each of **them** has a
separate management team.

Here the reference words function as follows:

MAZ	five divisions
it its	them

Examples of reference words and phrases:

Pronouns	he/she/it/they
Possessive pronouns	his/her/hers/its/their/theirs
Objective pronouns	her/him/them
Demonstrative pronouns	this/that/these/those
Other phrases	the former/the latter/the first/the second/such a

2 Practice exercise: Cohesion

■ Read the following paragraph and complete the table.

> **2.1**   **La Ferrera** (1997) has researched the life cycle **of new businesses.**
> **She** found that **they** have an **average life of only 4.7 years. This** is due to
> two main reasons; one **economic** and one **social. The former** appears to
> be a lack of capital, **the latte**r a failure to carry out sufficient market research.
> La Ferrera considers that together **these** account for approximately 70 per cent
> of business failures.

Reference	Reference word/phrase
La Ferrera	*She*
new businesses	
average life of only 4.7 years	
one economic	
one social	
the former . . . the latter . . .	

3 Avoiding confusion

To avoid confusing the reader it is important to use reference words only when the reference is clear. For example:

> **The company** was founded in 1953 and bought **the mine** in 1957. **It** was successful at first . . .

In this case it is not clear which noun (the company or the mine) 'It' refers to. So to avoid this write:

> **The company** was founded in 1953 and bought **the mine** in 1957. **The mine/the latter** was successful at first . . .

4 Practice exercise: Cohesion

■ In the following paragraph, insert suitable reference words from the box below in the gaps.

> **he / he / his / them / this / it / they**

4.1 GILLETTE'S BLADES

Disposable razor blades were invented in America by King Gillette at the beginning of the twentieth century. (a) _____ _____ was a simple idea, but at first (b) _____ found it very hard to sell (c) _____ . (d) _____ was because nobody had marketed a throw-away product before. However, (e) _____ use of advertising to stimulate demand gradually increased sales and (f) _____ became very popular. Within a few years (g) _____ was a millionaire.

5 Practice exercise: Cohesion

■ Read the paragraph below and replace as many nouns as possible with reference words, while keeping the meaning clear.

5.1 VELCRO

Velcro is a fabric fastener used with clothes and shoes. Velcro was invented by a Swiss engineer called George de Mestral. Mestral's idea was derived from studying the tiny hooks found on some plant seeds. The tiny hooks cling to animals and help disperse the seeds. Mestral spent eight years perfecting Mestral's invention, which Mestral called 'Velcro' from the French words 'velour' and 'crochet'. The invention was patented in 1955 and today over 60 million metres of Velcro are sold annually.

6 Practice exercise: Cohesion

■ Use the following information to write a paragraph about nylon, paying careful attention to the use of reference words.

Nylon

Inventor:	Wallace Carothers
Company:	DuPont Corporation (USA)
Carothers' position:	Director of research centre
Carothers' background:	Chemistry student, specialising in polymers (molecules composed of long chains of atoms)
Properties:	Strong but fine synthetic fibre
Patented:	1935
Mass produced:	1939
Applications:	Stockings, toothbrushes, parachutes, fishing lines, surgical thread

Comparisons

It is often necessary to make comparisons in academic writing. The comparison might be the subject of the essay, or might be given just to provide evidence for the argument. In all cases it is important to explain clearly what is being compared and to make the comparison as accurate as possible. This unit deals with different forms of comparison and practises their use.

1 Comparison structures

Some studies are based on a comparison:

> The purpose of this study is to compare Chinese and American consumers on their propensity to use self-service technology in a retail setting . . .

In other cases a comparison provides useful context:

> China's GDP in 2008 was $4.4 trillion, smaller than Japan's and less than a third of America's.

The two basic comparative forms are:

(a) France's economy is **larger** than Holland's

The students were **happier** after the exam

(-er is added to one-syllable adjectives and two-syllable adjectives ending in –y, which changes into an 'i')

(b) The Vietnamese economy is **more dynamic** than Malaysia's

(more . . . is used with other adjectives of two or more syllables)

These comparisons can be modified by the use of adverbs such as *slightly*, *considerably*, *significantly* and *substantially*:

(c) The Dutch economy is **slightly larger** than Australia's

Russia's GDP is **substantially smaller** than Mexico's

Similarity can be noted by the use of *as* . . . . *as*:

(d) France's population is **as numerous as** Britain's

The same form can be used for quantitative comparison:

Britain is half **as large as** France

(also twice as large as, ten times as fast as, etc.)

2 Practice exercise: Comparisons

■ Study the table on the next page, which shows the price of quality residential property in various cities. Complete the following comparisons, and write two more.

(a) Residential property in London is twice as expensive _____ in Rome.

(b) Property in Moscow is _____ cheaper than in New York.

(c) Tokyo property is nearly as expensive as property in _____ .

(d) Singapore has significantly cheaper property _____ New York.

Euros per sq. m.	City
28,000	London
16,500	New York
16,200	Moscow
16,000	Paris
15,850	Tokyo
13,500	Rome
11,850	Singapore
11,000	Sydney

(e) London is the _____ expensive of the eight cities, while Sydney is the cheapest.

(f) _____

   _____

   _____

(g) _____

   _____

   _____

3 Forms of comparison

Compare these three possible forms:

   Parisian property is more expensive than Roman (property).

   Property in Paris is more expensive than in Rome.

   The price of property in Paris is higher than in Rome.

Note that high/low are used for comparing abstract ideas (e.g. rates of inflation).

more/less must be used with *than + comparison*:

> Current unemployment is **less than last year's**

4 Using superlatives

When using superlatives take care to define the group, e.g. 'the cheapest car' has no meaning:

> the cheapest car **in the Ford range**/the fastest car **in the USA**

The most/the least are followed by an adjective:

> the **most interesting** example is Ireland . . .

The most/the fewest are used in relation to numbers:

> **the fewest** students studied insurance . . . (i.e. the lowest number)

5 Practice exercise: Comparisons

■ **Study the table, which shows the income of the top ten clubs in world football. Then read the comparisons. Each sentence contains one error. Find and correct it.**

Club	Revenue (million euros) 2007–8
Real Madrid	366
Manchester United	310
FC Barcelona	304
Bayern Munich	295
Chelsea	270
Arsenal	265
Liverpool	210
AC Milan	205
AS Roma	180
Internazionale	175

(a) Real Madrid was the richest club.

(b) Real Madrid's income was twice much as AS Roma's.

(c) FC Barcelona earned significantly less than Manchester United.

(d) Chelsea had a significantly better income than Liverpool.

(e) Internazionale had less revenue AC Milan.

6 Practice exercise: Comparisons

The table shows the per cent of GDP spent on health in a range of countries.

Country	Health spending as % of GDP
USA	14
Switzerland	11
Canada	9.5
South Africa	8.6
Denmark	8.4
Bangladesh	3.5
Oman	3.0
Indonesia	2.4
Madagascar	2.0
Azerbaijan	0.9

■ **Complete the gaps in the following paragraph (one word each).**

There are wide (a) _____ in the percentage of
GDP spent on health by different countries. The USA spends
14 per cent of GDP, (b) _____ times as much

as Bangladesh, and over five times (c) _____

much as Indonesia. South Africa (8.6 per cent) spends (d)

_____ more (e) _____ Denmark.

At the lower end, Madagascar only spends 2 per cent,

which is (f) _____ as much as Azerbaijan.

7 Practice exercise: Comparisons

The table below lists the wealthiest countries in the world by GDP per head, adjusted for PPP (purchasing power parity).

Rank	Country	GDP per head ($)
1	Luxembourg	78,500
2	Norway	58,100
3	Singapore	49,200
4	USA	46,700
5	Ireland	44,200
6	Switzerland	42,500
7	Netherlands	40,800
8	Austria	38,100
9	Sweden	37,400
10	Iceland	36,700

■ Write a paragraph comparing the countries.

> *The table shows the ten countries with the highest per-capita GDP, adjusted for PPP. The richest ...*

8 Practice exercise: Comparisons

The table below gives some data on two major UK supermarket chains.

	Annual turnover	Profits before tax	Operating margins	Market share	Number of employees	Number of stores
Sainsbury's	£20 bn.	£543 m.	3.3%	16%	150,000	792
Morrisons	£14.5 bn.	£359 m.	5.1%	12%	131,000	435

■ Write a paragraph comparing Sainsbury's and Morrisons.

> *The table compares ...*

Definitions

Definitions are usually found in introductions (see Unit 1.11). They are not needed in every case, but if the title includes an unfamiliar phrase, or if the writer wants to use a term in a special way, it is worth making clear to the reader exactly what is meant in this context. This unit presents ways of writing both simple and complex definitions.

1 Simple definitions

Basic definitions are formed by giving a category and the application:

Word	Category	Application
An agenda	is a set of issues	to be discussed in a meeting
A master's degree	is an academic award	for post-graduate students, given on completion of a dissertation

■ **Complete the following definitions by inserting a suitable category word or phrase:**

(a) A mortgage is a type of _____ used for buying property in which the lender has the security of the property.

(b) A multi-national company is a business _____
_____ that operates in many countries.

(c) A recession is a _____ of negative
economic growth.

(d) A cartel is an _____ between a
group of companies for the purpose of price-fixing.

(e) Overheads are the fixed _____ of
a business not related to production.

(f) A bull (colloquial) is an _____
with an optimistic economic outlook.

(g) A bond is a _____ offering a
fixed rate of return over a limited period.

■ **Write definitions for the following:**

(h) A trades union _____

_____

(i) A monopoly _____

_____

(j) Marketing _____

_____

(k) A dividend _____

_____

(l) A hostile takeover _____

_____

2 Complex definitions

■ **Study the following examples and underline the term being defined.**

(a) The definition for a failed project ranges from abandoned projects to projects that do not meet their full potential or simply have schedule overrun problems.

(b) Development is a socio-economic-technological process having the main objective of raising the standards of living of the people.

(c) Electronic commerce is characterised by an absence of physical proximity between the buyer and seller in conducting the search, assessment and transaction stages of a transaction.

(d) Corporate governance is a set of mechanisms, both institutional and market-based, designed to mitigate agency problems that arise from the separation of ownership and control in a company.

(e) Globalisation, in an economic sense, describes the opening up of national economies to global markets and global capital, the freer movement and diffusion of goods, services, finance, people, knowledge and technology around the world.

(f) Empathy as a concept has an interesting history. As Eisenberg and Strayer (1987) note: 'Some people take the term empathy to refer to a cognitive process analogous to cognitive role-taking (e.g. Deutsch and Madle, 1975); others take it to mean . . .'

These examples illustrate the variety of methods used in giving definitions.

■ **Which example(s)**

(i)   Gives a variety of relevant situations?

(ii)   Defines the term in a negative way?

(iii) Quotes a definition from another writer?

(iv)   Uses category words?

(v)   Explains a process?

3 Practice exercise: Definitions

When writing introductions it is often useful to define a term in the title, even if it is fairly common, in order to demonstrate your understanding of its meaning.

■ **Study the following titles, underline the terms that are worth defining, and write a definition for three of them.**

(a) Do 'managing diversity' policies and practices in HRM add value?

(b) How can the management of an entrepreneurial business retain its entrepreneurial culture as it matures?

(c) Why is organisational culture of sustained interest not only for academics but also for practising managers?

(d) Is it true that firms in perfect competition do not make a profit?

1
2
3

Examples

Examples are used in academic writing for support and illustration. Suitable examples can strengthen the argument, but they can also help the reader to understand a point. This unit demonstrates the different ways in which examples can be introduced, and practises their use.

1 Using examples

Generalisations are commonly used to introduce a topic:

> It is often claimed that many mergers are unsuccessful . . .

But if the reader is given an example for illustration the idea becomes more concrete:

> It is often claimed that many mergers are unsuccessful, **for instance the merger between Compaq and Hewlett-Packard in 2005** . . .

The example may also support the point the writer is making:

> . . . in recent years researchers have begun looking into corporate governance in transition economies . . . For example,

Djankov and Murrell (2002) document that more than 150,000 large SOEs in transition economies have undergone enterprise restructuring ...

■ **Which of the following use examples for support and which for illustration?**

(a) The use of incentive compensation, **such as bonus and stock options**, is an important means of motivating and compensating executives of private companies, **especially executives of technology-orientated companies.**

(b) Earlier studies have also documented that the cost of holding an under-diversified portfolio can be substantial. **For example, Peters (1991) shows how differential diversification abilities of managers ...**

(c) Other consumers, however, intentionally avoid such self-service technologies. **For example, some retailers who are using in-store internet kiosks have found that not all consumers are interested in using the new technology (Mearin, 2001).**

▶ See Unit 2.7 Generalisations

2 Phrases to introduce examples

(a) for instance, for example (with commas)

Some car manufacturers, for instance Hyundai, now offer five-year guarantees ...

(b) such as, e.g.

Many entrepreneurs, such as Bill Gates, have no formal qualifications ...

(c) particularly, especially (to give a focus)

Certain MBA courses, especially American ones, take two years ...

(d) a case in point (for single examples)

A few countries have experienced deflation. A case in point is Japan ...

■ **Add a suitable example to each sentence and introduce it with one of the phrases above.**

Example:

Certain industries are experiencing labour shortages.

Certain industries, **for instance engineering,** are experiencing labour shortages.

(a) Some twentieth-century inventions affected the lives of most people.

(b) A number of sports have become very profitable due to the sale of television rights.

(c) Various companies have built their reputation on the strength of one product.

(d) Some brands have remained successful for more than 50 years.

(e) In recent years the product life cycle has tended to become shorter.

(f) A variety of products are promoted by celebrity endorsement.

(g) Speculation in some commodities has created price bubbles.

(h) Investors are often advised to spread their risk by putting their money into a range of investments.

3 Practice exercise: Examples

■ **Read the text below and then insert suitable examples where needed.**

3.1 Students who go to study abroad often experience a type of culture shock when they arrive in the new country. Customs which they took for granted in their own society may not be followed in the host country. Even everyday patterns of life may be different. When these are added to the inevitable differences which occur in every country students may at first feel confused. They may experience rapid changes of mood, or even want to return home. However, most soon make new friends and, in a relatively short period, are able to adjust to their new environment. They may even find that they prefer some aspects of their new surroundings, and forget that they are not at home for a while!

4 Restatement

Another small group of phrases is used when there is only one 'example'.
This is a kind of restatement:

> The world's leading gold producer, i.e. South Africa, has been
> faced with a number of technical difficulties.

in other words   namely   that is (to say)   i.e.   viz (very formal)

■ **Add a suitable phrase from the box below to the following sentences,**
  to make them clearer.

(a) The company's overheads doubled last year.

(b) During a bear market few investors make money.

(c) The Indian capital has a thriving commercial centre.

(d) The last day of the 2008–9 financial year was a Tuesday.

i.e. 31 March in other words the fixed costs that is, a period of falling share prices namely New Delhi

Generalisations

Generalisations are often used to introduce a topic. They can be powerful statements because they are simple and easy to understand. But they must be used with care, to avoid being overly simplistic or inaccurate. This unit explains how to generalise clearly and correctly.

1 Using generalisations

Generalisations are used to give a simple picture of a topic. Compare:

> 54.9 per cent of Spanish companies employ fewer than 10 people.

> The majority of Spanish companies employ fewer than 10 people.

Although the first sentence is more accurate, the second is easier to understand and remember. The writer must decide when accuracy is necessary, and when a generalisation will be acceptable. For example, the graph on the following page shows a stock market's performance during one day.

For most purposes, it is adequate to generalise the performance as:

> The FTSE 100 index fell 40 points on November 23rd.

This ignores the hour-by-hour changes but gives an overall picture.

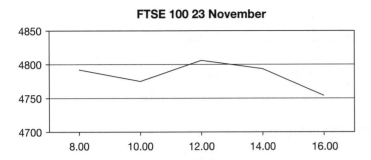

2 Structure

Generalisations can be made in two ways:

(a) most commonly using the plural:

Joint stock companies began in the sixteenth century.

(b) using the singular + definite article (more formal):

The joint stock company began in the sixteenth century.

Avoid absolute phrases in generalisations such as:

Small companies adapt faster to changing markets.

Instead, it is better to use cautious phrases such as:

Small companies tend to adapt faster to changing markets.

▶ **See Unit 3.4 Caution**

■ **Write generalisations on the following topics.**

(a) Market research/new products;

   Example: Market research can be vital for evaluating new
                    products.

(b) Job satisfaction/rates of pay: _____

_____

(c) Weak currency/level of exports: _____

_____

(d) Spending on R & D/introduction of new products: _____

_____

(e) Unemployment/level of consumer spending: _____

_____

(f) Cold weather/demand for gas: _____

_____

3 Over-generalising

This means making statements that are too simple or inaccurate. For example, using income figures from the table below, a writer might claim:

People were much richer in 2009 than 20 years earlier.

This ignores inflation over the period. It is more accurate to say:

Average incomes doubled between 1989 and 2009.

Comparison of some key economic indicators for the UK, 1989–2009

Britain	1989	1999	2009
Inflation rate	7.8%	3.4%	1.9%
Interest rate	13.7%	5.5%	0.5%
Unemployment	6.1%	4.6%	7.8%
Average income	£11,700	£19,000	£24,000
Average house price	£61,500	£68,300	£160,000

■ Some of the following sentences are accurate, but others are over-generalised. Rewrite the latter more accurately.

(a) The average price of houses more than doubled between 1999 and 2009.

(b) In the 20 years 1989–2009, the peak of unemployment was in 2009.

(c) 2009 was the worst year for savers.

(d) In relation to income, houses were cheaper in 1999 than 2009.

(e) The UK rate of inflation fell steadily from 1989 to 2009.

4 Practice exercise: Generalisations

■ Read the following text and write five generalisations using the information.

4.1   **ENCOURAGING ENTREPRENEURSHIP**

Many countries have attempted to copy the example of Silicon Valley in California and tried to create their own entrepreneurial centres of new technology. However, these attempts are rarely successful, partly because they ignore the reasons why the original was so outstanding: being close to two first-class universities and a major financial centre.

Three patterns for developing entrepreneurial powerhouses have been identified. The first is where a major company stimulates the growth of surrounding smaller firms. Another can occur when a recession creates widespread redundancy among skilled workers, who use their knowledge to create a cluster of new businesses. Finally, a successful local businessman or woman may build an enterprise that creates opportunities for others.

But two other ingredients can affect results: chance and culture. If the culture is filled with barriers to business development, the more enterprising are likely to take their ideas to somewhere more suitable, as many Indians did in the 1960s and 70s.

(a) _____

_____

(b) _____

_____

(c) _____

_____

(d) _____

_____

(e) _____

_____

5 Building on generalisations

Most essays move from the general to the specific, as a generalisation has to be supported and developed. For example, an essay with the title 'The impact of globalisation on the Chinese economy' might develop in this way:

Generalisation	Support	Development > Specific
Since the mid-twentieth century there has been a remarkable increase in international trade.	The reasons for this are a combination of international agreements such as GATT, better transport and improved communications.	China has played a significant part in this process, with its international trade growing by 16 times in just 20 years, while its GDP increased by nearly 10% per year.

■ **Choose a title from the list below, write a generalisation and develop it in the same way.**

(a) People are often positively disposed to their own country's products – Discuss.

(b) To what extent has management theory made space for gender?

(c) Evaluate the contribution of Small and Medium Enterprises (SMEs) to the economy.

(d) Compare and contrast the challenges facing big business groups in China, Japan and South Korea.

Generalisation	Support	Development > Specific

2.8 **Numbers**

Business and Economics students need to be able to write about statistical data clearly and accurately. Presenting statistics in charts and tables is dealt with in Unit 2.11 Visual information, while this unit explains and practises the basic language of numbers and percentages.

1 The language of numbers

In introductions numbers are often used to give an accurate account of a situation:

> Women account for fewer than 2 per cent of Fortune 500 CEOs, 14 per cent of Fortune 500 directors, and 8 per cent and 5 per cent of board directors and top managers, respectively, of the biggest west European companies.

> If the family holds 50 per cent of the shares in firm A and firm A holds 50 per cent of the shares in firm B, the family holds 25 per cent (0.5 times 0.5) of the cash flow rights in firm B but controls 50 per cent of the votes in that firm.

Figures and **numbers** are both used to talk about statistical data in a general sense.

> The **figures/numbers** in the report need to be read critically.

Digits are individual numbers.

4,539 – a four **digit** number

Both **fractions** (½) and **decimals** (0.975) may be used.

There is no final 's' on hundred/thousand/million used with whole numbers:

six **million** people live there

but: **thousands of** companies were formed in the dotcom boom

When writing about **currencies** write $440 m. or four hundred and forty million dollars.

Rates are normally expressed as percentages (e.g. the rate of inflation fell to 2.5 per cent) but may also be per thousand (e.g. the Austrian birth rate is 8.7)

It is normal to write whole numbers as words from one to ten and as digits above ten:

Five people normally work in the café, but at peak times this can rise to 14.

2 Percentages

These are commonly used for expressing degrees of change:

Between 2003 and 2005 the number of female managers rose by 10 per cent.

■ **Complete the following sentences using the data in the table below.**

(a) Between 2007 and 2008, the number of overseas students increased by _____ per cent.

(b) The number increased by _____ per cent the following year.

(c) Between 2007 and 2010 there was a _____ per cent increase.

Overseas students in the university 2007–2010

2007	2008	2009	2010
200	300	600	1000

3 Simplification

Although the accurate use of numbers is vital, too many statistics can make texts difficult to read. If the actual number is not important, words such as *various, dozens* or *scores* may be used instead:

53 employees opted for voluntary redundancy.

Dozens of employees opted for voluntary redundancy.

few	less than expected
a few	approximately 3–6 depending on context
several	approximately 3–4
various	approximately 4–6
dozens of	approximately 30–60
scores of	approximately 60–100

■ **Rewrite the following sentences using one of the words or phrases in the table above.**

Example:

(a) Only three people attended the meeting.

Few people attended the meeting

(b) 77 students applied for the scholarship.

(c) He rewrote the essay three times.

(d) 54 books were published on the economic crisis.

(e) Five names were suggested but rejected for the new chocolate bar.

4 Practice exercise: Numbers

The expressions listed below can also be used to present and simplify statistical information. For example:

> The price of coffee rose from $750 to $1,550 in two years.
>
> The price of coffee doubled in two years.

If appropriate, roughly/approximately can be added:

> The price of coffee roughly doubled in two years.

one in three	**one in three** new businesses ceases trading within a year
twice/three times as many	**twice as many** women as men study business law
a five/tenfold increase	there was **a fivefold increase** in the price of oil
to double/halve	the rate of inflation **halved** after 1997
the highest/lowest	**the lowest** rate of home ownership was in Germany
a quarter/fifth	**a fifth** of all employees leave every year
the majority/minority	**the majority** of shareholders supported the board
on average, the average	**on average**, each salesperson sells four cars a week
a small/large proportion	the website generates **a large proportion** of their sales

NB.5–20 per cent = a tiny/small minority
    40–49 per cent = a substantial/significant minority
    51–55 per cent = a small majority
    80 per cent + = a vast majority

■ **Rewrite each sentence in a simpler way, using a suitable expression from the list above.**

(a) In 1975 a litre of petrol cost 12p, while the price is now £1.20.

(b) Out of eighteen students in the group twelve were women.

(c) The new high-speed train reduced the journey time to Madrid from seven hours to three hours 20 minutes.

(d) The number of students applying for the Management course has risen from 350 last year to 525 this year.

(e) Visitor numbers to the theme park show a steady increase. In 2007 there were 40,000 admissions, in 2008 82,000 and 171,000 in 2009.

(f) More than 80 per cent of British students complete their first degree course; in Italy the figure is just 35 per cent.

(g) Tap water costs 0.07p per litre while bottled water costs, on average, 50p per litre.

(h) The rate of unemployment ranges from 18 per cent in Spain to 3 per cent in Norway.

(i) 27 out of every hundred garments produced had some kind of fault.

(j) 57 per cent of shareholders supported the proposal, but 83 per cent of these expressed some doubts.

5 Practice exercise: Numbers

■ **The data in the table on the following page was collected about a group of 15 international students. Write sentences about the group using the data.**

(a) _____

_____

(b) _____

_____

(c) _____

_____

(d) _____

_____

(e) _____

_____

(f) _____

_____

Mother tongue		Future course		Age		Favourite sport	
Arabic	2	Accounting	1	21	1	climbing	2
Chinese	8	Economics	3	22	3	cycling	1
French	1	Finance	2	23	9	dancing	3
Japanese	1	Management	6	24	-	football	3
Korean	2	MBA	2	25	-	swimming	5
Spanish	1	Tourism	1	26	1	tennis	1

Problems and solutions

Writing tasks frequently ask students to examine a problem and evaluate a range of solutions. This unit explains ways in which this kind of text can be organised. Note that some of the language is similar to that practised in Unit 2.1 Argument and discussion.

1 Structure

■ Study the organisation of the following paragraph:

1.1 ROAD CONGESTION

Currently, roads are often congested, which is expensive in terms of delays to the movement of people and freight. It is commonly suggested that building more roads, or widening existing ones, would ease the traffic jams. But not only is the cost of such work high, but the construction process adds to the congestion, while the resulting extra road space may encourage extra traffic. Therefore constructing more road space is unlikely to solve the problem, and other remedies, such as road pricing or greater use of public transport, should be examined.

(a) Problem	Currently, roads are often congested, which is . . .
(b) Solution A	It is commonly suggested that building more roads, or widening . . .
(c) Arguments against solution A	But not only is the cost of such work high, but . . .
(d) Solutions B and C	. . . other remedies, such as road pricing or greater use . . .

2 Alternative structure

The same ideas could be re-ordered to arrive at a different conclusion:

2.1   **ROAD CONGESTION**

Currently, roads are often congested, which is expensive in terms of delays to the movement of people and freight. It is commonly suggested that building more roads, or widening existing ones, would ease the traffic jams. This remedy is criticised for being expensive and liable to lead to more road use. This may be partly true, yet the alternatives are equally problematic. Road pricing has many practical difficulties, while people are reluctant to use public transport. There is little alternative to a road building programme except increasing road chaos.

Problem	Currently, roads are often congested, which is . . .
Solution A	It is commonly suggested that building more roads, or widening . . .
Arguments against solution A	This remedy is criticised for being expensive . . .
Solutions B and C and arguments against	Road pricing has many practical difficulties, while people are . . .
Conclusion in favour of solution A	There is little alternative to a road building programme . . .

3 Practice exercise: Problems and solutions

■ Analyse the following paragraph in a similar way:

3.1   **MANAGING TOURISM GROWTH**

Many developing countries have found that the development of a tourism industry can bring social and environmental drawbacks. Growing visitor numbers can cause pollution and put pressure on scarce resources such as water. One possible solution is to target upmarket holidaymakers, in order to get the maximum profit from minimum numbers. However, this is a limited market and requires considerable investment in infrastructure and training. Another remedy is to rigorously control the environmental standards of any development, in order to minimise the impact of the construction. This requires effective government agencies, but is likely to ensure the best outcome for both tourists and locals.

Problem	
Solution A	
Argument against solution A	
Solution B	
Conclusion in favour of B	

4 Vocabulary

The following words can be used as synonyms for *problem* and *solution*.

three main **difficulties** have arisen . . .	the best **remedy** for this may be . . .
the main **challenge** faced by SMEs . . .	two **answers** have been put forward . . .
one of the **concerns** during the recession . . .	another **suggestion** is . . .
the new process created two **questions** . . .	Matheson's **proposal** was finally accepted.
our principal **worry** was . . .	

5 Practice exercise: Problems and solutions

■ **Use the following points to build an argument in one paragraph, using the box below.**

Topic:	University expansion
Problem:	Demand for university places is growing, leading to overcrowding in lectures and seminars
Solution A:	Increase fees to reduce demand
Argument against A:	Unfair to poorer students
Solution B:	Government pays to expand universities
Argument against B:	Unfair to average taxpayer who would be subsidising the education of a minority who will earn high salaries
Conclusion:	Government should subsidise poorer students

University expansion

Currently there is increasing demand . . .

6 Practice exercise: Problems and solutions

■ Think of a similar problem in your subject area. Complete the table and
write a paragraph that leads to a conclusion.

Topic	
Problem	
Solution A	
Argument against A	
Solution B	
Argument against B	
(Solution C)	
Conclusion	

Style

There is no one correct style of academic writing, and students should aim to develop their own 'voice'. In general, it should attempt to be accurate, impersonal and objective. In order to present information and ideas as clearly as possible a rather formal vocabulary is used. Personal pronouns like 'I' and idioms are used less often than in other writing. This unit gives some guidelines for an appropriate style, but see also Units 3.4 on Caution and 3.13 on Passives.

1 A suitable academic style

■ Study this paragraph and underline any examples of poor style.

| 1.1 | How to make people work harder is a topic that lots of people have written about in the last few years. There are lots of different theories etc and I think some of them are ok. When we think about this we should remember the old Chinese proverb, that you can lead a horse to water but you can't make it drink. So how do we increase production? It's quite a complex subject but I'll just talk about a couple of ideas. |

Some of the problems with the style of this paragraph can be analysed as follows:

How to make people work harder . . .	Imprecise vocabulary – use 'motivation'
. . . lots of people . . .	Vague – give names
. . . the last few years	Vague – give dates
lots of different . . .	Avoid 'lots of'
. . . etc . . .	Avoid using 'etc' and 'so on'
. . . I think . . .	Too personal
. . . are ok	Too informal
When we think about this . . .	Too personal
. . . the old Chinese proverb . . .	Do not quote proverbs or similar expressions
So how do we increase production?	Avoid rhetorical questions
It's quite a . . .	Avoid contractions
. . . I'll just talk about a couple . . .	Too personal and informal

The paragraph could be rewritten:

1.2 Motivation has been the subject of numerous studies during recent decades, but this essay will focus on Maslow's hierarchy of needs theory (1943) and Herzberg's two-factor theory (1966). Their contemporary relevance to the need to motivate employees effectively will be examined critically, given that this can be considered crucial to a firm's survival in the current economic climate.

2 Guidelines

There are no rules for academic style that apply to all situations. The following are guidelines, which should help you develop a style of your own.

(a) Do not use idiomatic or colloquial vocabulary, e.g. *kids, boss*. Instead use standard English: *children, manager*.

(b) Use vocabulary accurately. There is a difference between *currency* and *money*, or *governance* and *government*, which you are expected to know.

(c) Be as precise as possible when dealing with facts or figures. Avoid phrases such as *about a hundred* or *hundreds of years ago*. If it is necessary to estimate numbers use *approximately* rather than *about*.

(d) Conclusions should use tentative language. Avoid absolute statements such as *unemployment causes crime*. Instead use cautious phrases: *unemployment may cause crime* or *tends to cause crime*.

(e) Avoid adverbs that show your personal attitude, e.g. *luckily, remarkably, surprisingly*.

(f) Do not contract verb forms, e.g. *don't, can't*. Use the full form: *do not, cannot*.

(g) Although academic English tends to use the passive more than standard English, it should not be over-used. Both have their place. Compare:

Manners (1995) claims that most companies perform worse when . . .

It is widely agreed that most companies perform worse when . . .

In the first case, the focus is on the source, in the second on what companies do.

(h) Avoid the following:

- *like* for introducing examples – use *such as* or *for instance*.

- *thing* and combinations *nothing* or *something* – use *factor, issue* or *topic*.

- *lots of* – use *a significant/considerable number*.

- *little/big* – use *small/large*.

- 'get' phrases such as *get better/worse* – use *improve* and *deteriorate*.

- *good/bad* are simplistic – use *positive/negative*, e.g. *the changes had several positive aspects*

(i) Do not use question forms such as *What were the reasons for the decline in wool exports?* Instead use statements: *There were four main reasons for the decline . . .*

(j) Avoid numbering sections of your text, except in reports and long essays. Use conjunctions and signposting expressions to introduce new sections, e.g. *Turning to the question of taxation . . .*

(k) When writing lists, avoid using *etc.* or *and so on*. Insert *and* before the last item, e.g. *The main products were pharmaceuticals, electronic goods and confectionery.*

(l) Avoid using two-word verbs such as *go on* or *bring up* if there is a suitable synonym – use *continue* or *raise*.

3 Practice exercise: Style

■ **In the following sentences, underline examples of bad style and rewrite them in a more suitable way.**

(a) What was the biggest thing that made Enron collapse?

(b) Unfortunately, I think there's a good chance of inflation increasing.

(c) Lots of people think that the economy is getting worse.

(d) A few years ago the price of property in Japan went down a lot.

(e) You can't always trust the numbers in that report.

(f) Sadly, the Russian inflation led to poverty, social unrest and so on.

(g) They sacked the boss for cooking the books.

(h) These days lots of people don't have jobs.

4 Avoiding repetition and redundancy

Repetition means repeating a word instead of using a synonym to provide variety. So instead of:

> Most family businesses employ less than ten people. These businesses . . .

Use:

> Most family businesses employ less than ten people. These **firms** . . .

▶ **See Unit 3.11 Synonyms**

Redundancy, i.e. repeating an idea or including an irrelevant point, suggests that the writer is not fully in control of the material. It gives the impression that either he does not properly understand the language or is trying to 'pad' the essay by repeating the same point. Avoid phrases such as:

> Business schools in Spain are cheaper than business schools in the UK.

> Homelessness is a global problem in the whole world.

Good writing aims for economy and precision:

> Business schools in Spain are cheaper than in the UK.

> Homelessness is a global problem.

■ **In the following text, remove all repetition and redundancy, rewriting where necessary.**

4.1   **FAST FOOD**

Currently these days, fast food is growing in popularity. Fast food is a kind of food that people can buy or cook quickly. This essay examines the advantages of fast food and the drawbacks of fast food. First above all, fast food is usually tasty. Most of the people who work in offices are very busy, so that they do not have time to go to their homes for lunch. But the people who work in offices can eat tasty and delicious food in McDonalds' restaurants, which are franchised in hundreds of countries. In addition, the second benefit of fast food is its cheapness. As it is produced in large quantities, this high volume means that the companies can keep costs down. As a result fast food is usually less expensive than a meal in a conventional restaurant.

5 Varying sentence length

Short sentences are clear and easy to read:

> Car scrappage schemes have been introduced in many countries.

But too many short sentences are monotonous:

> Car scrappage schemes have been introduced in many countries. They offer a subsidy to buyers of new cars. The buyers must scrap an old vehicle. The schemes are designed to stimulate the economy. They also increase fuel efficiency.

Long sentences are more interesting but can be difficult to construct and read:

> Car scrappage schemes, which offer a subsidy to buyers of new cars, who must scrap an old vehicle, have been introduced in many countries; the schemes are designed to stimulate the economy and also increase fuel efficiency.

Effective writing normally uses a mixture of long and short sentences.

■ **(a) Rewrite the following paragraph so that instead of six short sentences there are two long and two short sentences.**

Worldwide, enrolments in higher education are increasing. In developed countries over half of all young people enter college. Similar trends are seen in China and South America. This growth has put financial strain on state university systems. Many countries are asking students and parents to contribute. This leads to a debate about whether students or society benefit from tertiary education.

■ (b) The following sentence is too long. Divide it into shorter ones.

> **5.1**   China is one developing country (but not the only one)
>   which has imposed fees on students since 1997, but
> the results have been surprising: enrolments, especially in the
> most expensive universities, have continued to rise steeply,
> growing 200 per cent overall between 1997 and 2001; it seems
> in this case that higher fees attract rather than discourage
> students, who see them as a sign of a good education, and
> compete more fiercely for places, leading to the result that a
> place at a good college can cost $5000 per year for fees and
> maintenance.

Until you feel confident in your writing, it is better to use shorter rather than longer sentences. This should make your meaning as clear as possible.

Visual information

In many assignments in Business and Economics it is essential to support your points with statistics. Visual devices such as graphs and tables are a convenient way of displaying large quantities of information in a form that is easy to understand. This unit explains and practises the language connected with these devices.

1 The language of change

Verb ↗	Adverb	Verb ↘	Adjective + noun
grew	slightly	dropped	a slight drop
rose	gradually	fell	a gradual fall
increased	steadily	decreased	a sharp decrease
climbed	sharply		
also: a peak, to peak, a plateau, to level off, a trough			

Profit margins **grew steadily** until 2006 and then **dropped slightly**.

There was a **sharp decrease** in sales during the summer and then a **gradual rise**.

■ **Study the graph below and complete the description with phrases from the table above.**

The graph shows that inflation (a) _____ slightly between January and February and then (b) _____ until April. It subsequently climbed (c)_____ to July, when it (d) _____ at just over 5 per cent. From July to September inflation (e) _____ steeply.

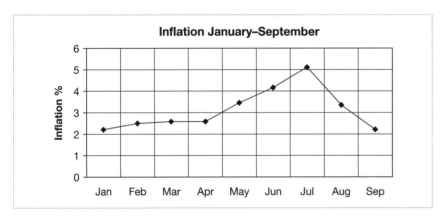

2 Practice exercise: Visual information

■ **Below (pp. 156–157) are examples of some of the main types of visuals used in academic texts. Complete the box below to show the use (a)–(f) and the example (A)–(F) of each type.**

Uses:

(a) location

(b) comparison

(c) proportion

(d) function

(e) changes in time

(f) statistical display

TYPES	USES	EXAMPLE
1 diagram		
2 table		
3 map		
4 pie chart		
5 bar chart		
6 line graph		

(A) Cinema ticket sales

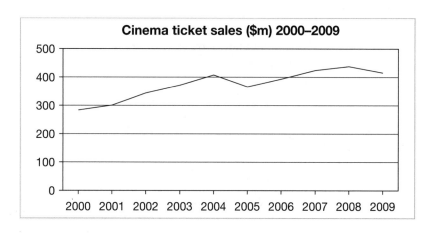

Cinema ticket sales ($m) 2000–2009

(B) Total expenditure on R & D (% of GDP)

Sweden	3.6
Finland	3.4
Iceland	3.1
Japan	3.0
South Korea	2.9
United States	2.8
Switzerland	2.6

(C) Electricity output
    from coal

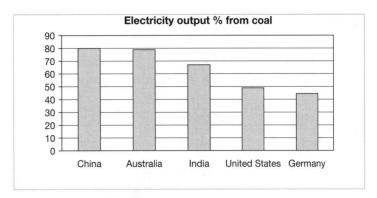

(D) Origins of international
    students

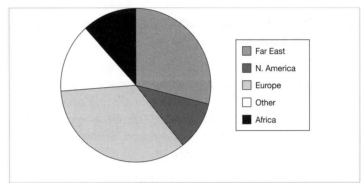

(E) Structure of the
    research unit

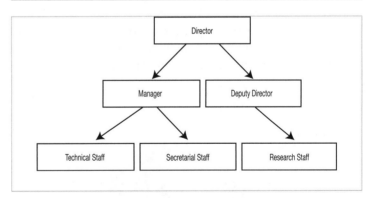

(F) Position of the main
    library

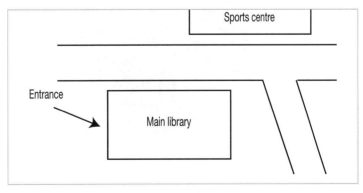

3 Describing visuals

Although visuals do largely speak for themselves, it is common to help the reader interpret them by briefly commenting on their main features.

The graph	shows	the changes in the price of oil since 1990
map	illustrates	the main sources of copper in Africa
diagram	displays	the organisation of both companies

■ (a) **Read the following descriptions of the chart below. Which is better?**

(i) The chart shows the quantity of tea consumed by the world's leading tea consuming nations. India and China together consume more than half the world's tea production, with India alone consuming about one third. Other significant tea consumers are Turkey, Russia and Britain. 'Others' includes the United States, Iran and Egypt.

(ii) The chart shows that 31 per cent of the world's tea is consumed by India, 23 per cent by China, and 8 per cent by Turkey. The fourth largest consumers are Russia, Japan and Britain, with 7 per cent each, while Pakistan consumes 5 per cent. Other countries account for the remaining 12 per cent.

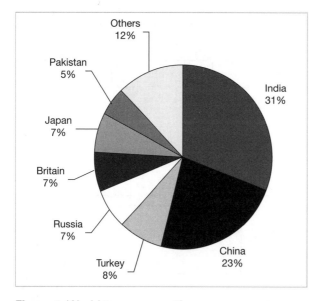

(Source: The Tea Council)

Figure 1 World tea consumption

■ **(b) Complete the description of the chart below.**

The bar chart shows population (a) _____ in a
variety of countries around the world. It (b) _____
the extreme contrast (c) _____ crowded
nations such as South Korea (475 people per sq. km.) and
much (d) _____ countries such as Canada
(three people per sq. km.). Clearly, climate plays a major
(e) _____ in determining population
density, (f) _____ the least crowded nations
(g) _____ to have extreme climates (e.g. cold in Russia
or dry in Algeria).

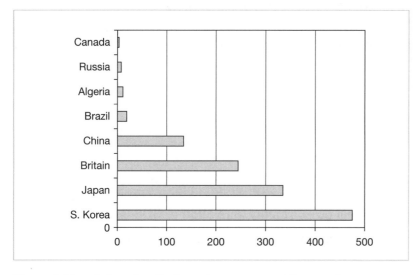

(Source:
OECD)

Figure 2 Population density (people per square kilometre)

4 Labelling

- When referring to visual information in the text, the word 'figure' is used for almost everything (such as maps, charts and graphs) except tables. Figures and tables should be numbered and given a title. Titles of tables are written above, while titles of figures are written below the data. As with other data, sources must be given for all visual information.

- If you are writing a lengthy work such as a dissertation you will need to provide lists of tables and figures, showing numbers, titles and page numbers after the contents page.

5 Practice exercise: Visual information

■ Complete the following description of the table below (one word per gap).

Table 1 Government taxation 2007

	Australia	Brazil	China	France	Germany	India	Japan	Russia	UK	USA
Total tax as % GDP	29.5	32.3	16.4	44.7	40.4	18.9	28.2	33.2	37.7	28.0

Source: OECD

Table 1 (a) _____ the proportion of tax revenues raised by national governments in relation to GDP in 2007. It can be seen that there are considerable variations, with the (b) _____ government collecting nearly 45 per cent of GDP, while in China the (c)_____ is below 20 per cent. In general, (d) _____ with higher welfare spending such as France, Germany and the UK collect more (e) _____ the developing BRIC economies such as India, but there are some exceptions to this, with the Brazilian government collecting a (f) _____ percentage of GDP than Australia's.

6 Practice exercise: Visual information

■ Write a paragraph commenting on the data in the table below.

Table 2 The world's largest companies 2008

Rank	Company	Revenues $m.	Profits $m.
1.	Royal Dutch Shell	458,361	26,277
2.	Exxon Mobile	442,851	45,220
3.	Wal-Mart Stores	405,607	13,400
4.	BP	367,053	21,157
5.	Chevron	263,159	23,931
6.	Total	234,674	15,500
7.	Conoco Phillips	230,764	−16,998
8.	ING Group	226,577	−1,067
9.	Synopec	207,814	1,961
10.	Toyota Motor	204,352	−4,349

Source: *Fortune* magazine

Working in groups

Many courses in business schools expect students to complete assignments as part of a group of four to eight students. This unit explains the reasons for this, and suggests the best way to approach group work in order to achieve the maximum benefit from the process.

1 Group work

■ **Read the text on p. 163. Working in pairs, decide if the following are true or false.**

(a) Most students react positively to the idea of group work.

(b) All the group members receive the same mark.

(c) Students in groups can normally choose who they work with.

(d) There are two main reasons for setting group work.

(e) Most employers look for successful team members.

(f) Group work in business school has no connection to team work in companies.

1.1   THE IMPORTANCE OF GROUP WORK IN THE BUSINESS SCHOOL

Some students in business schools, especially those from other academic cultures, may be surprised to find they are expected to work in groups to complete some academic assignments. For those who have always worked on their own this may cause a kind of culture shock, especially as all the students in the group will normally be given the same mark for the group's work. In addition, students are normally told who they will work with, although the group may be able to choose its own topic with some kinds of project. However, there are important reasons for this emphasis on group work in many English-speaking institutions.

First of all, employers are generally looking for people who can work in a team. Most companies don't want brilliant individuals, instead they want employees who are comfortable working with a mixed group with different skills and backgrounds. So teamwork has become an essential qualification for many jobs, and this task provides students with an opportunity to strengthen their experience of working in groups.

Furthermore, working in groups allows individuals to achieve more than they could by working on their own. A group can tackle much larger projects, and this applies to most research work at university, as well as business development in companies. Finally, by taking part in these activities students are able to provide evidence on their portfolio and CV that they have succeeded in this critical area.

2 Making group work successful

Below is a list of suggestions for making your group work successful. The
correct order (1–7) has been mixed up.

■ **Working with a partner, put them into the most logical sequence, using
the box below.**

Analyse the task
Get everyone to discuss the assignment and agree on the best
methods to complete it. At this stage it is important to have
complete agreement on the objectives.

Divide up the work fairly, according to the abilities of the members
Your group may include a computer expert or a design genius,
so make sure that their talents are used for the benefit of the
task. It is most important to make sure that everyone feels they
have been given a fair share of the work.

Make everyone feel included
Nobody should feel an outsider, so make special efforts if there
is only one male student, or one non-native speaker, for
instance. Make a list of all members' phone numbers and
email addresses and give everyone a copy.

Finish the assignment on time
This is the most important test of your group's performance.
When you have finished and handed in your work, it may be
helpful to have a final meeting to discuss what you have all
learned from the task.

Get to know the other members
Normally you cannot choose who you work with, so it is
crucial to introduce yourselves before starting work. Meet
informally in a café or similar (but be careful not to choose a
meeting place that may make some members uncomfortable,
such as a bar).

Select a co-ordinator/editor
Someone needs to take notes about what was agreed at
meetings and send these to all members as a reminder. The
same person could also act as editor, to make sure that all the
individual sections conform to the same layout and format.
However, you should all be responsible for proof-reading your
own work.

Plan the job and the responsibilities
Break down the task week by week and allocate specific roles
to each member. Agree on times for regular meetings –
although you may be able to avoid some meetings by using
group emails. You may want to book a suitable room, for
example in the library, to hold your meetings.

1	
2	
3	
4	
5	*Divide up the work fairly, according to the abilities of the members.*
6	
7	

3 Dealing with problems

■ **Working in groups of three, discuss the best response to the following situations. You may choose an alternative strategy to the ones provided.**

(a) In a group of six, you find that two students are not doing any
work. Not only do they not come to meetings, they have not
done the tasks they were given at the beginning. Should you
. . .

   (i)   decide that it's simplest to do the work of the missing
          students yourself?

   (ii)   find the students and explain that their behaviour is going
          to damage the chances of all six members?

   (iii) tell your lecturer about the problem?

(b) You are the only non-native speaker in the group. Although you can understand normal speech, the other students speak so fast and idiomatically that you have difficulty taking part in the discussions. Should you . . .

   (i)   tell your lecturer about the problem?

   (ii)   keep quiet and ask another student in the group to explain decisions later?

   (iii)   explain your problem to the group and ask them to speak more slowly?

(c) One member of the group is very dominant. He/she attempts to control the group and is intolerant of the opinions of others. Should you . . .

   (i)   explain to them, in a group meeting, that their behaviour is having a negative effect on the group's task?

   (ii)   tell your lecturer about the problem?

   (iii)   let them do all the work, because that's what they seem to want?

4 Points to remember

Finally, remember that:

- working in groups is an ideal opportunity to make new friends – make the most of it

- you may learn a lot by listening to other people's ideas

- negotiation is important in a group – nobody is right all the time

- you should respect the values and attitudes of others, especially people from different cultures – you may be surprised what you learn

Accuracy in writing

PART 3

Abbreviations

Abbreviations are an important and expanding feature of contemporary English, widely used for convenience and space-saving. Students need to be familiar with general, academic and business abbreviations.

1 Types of abbreviation

Abbreviations take the form of shortened words, acronyms or other abbreviations, as shown below.

(a) **Shortened words** are often used without the writer being aware of the original form. 'Ad' and 'advert' come from 'advertisement', which is rarely used in modern English. However, 'refrigerator' is still better in written English than the informal 'fridge'. 'Public house' is now very formal ('pub' is acceptable), but 'television' or 'TV' should be used instead of the idiomatic 'telly'.

(b) **Acronyms** are made up of the initial letters of a name or phrase (e.g. SWOT = Strengths, Weaknesses, Opportunities, Threats). They are pronounced as words.

(c) **Other abbreviations** are read as sets of individual letters. They include names of countries, organisations and companies (USA/BBC/IBM), and also abbreviations that are only found in written English (e.g. PTO means 'please turn over'). Note that in many cases abbreviations are widely used without most users knowing what the individual letters stand for (e.g. DNA, ABS).

2 Business abbreviations

As with all academic subjects, Business and Economics employ abbreviations to save time and space. Common examples include:

AGM	annual general meeting
B2B	business to business
CEO	chief executive officer
CV	curriculum vitae
DIY	do-it-yourself (retail sector)
EPS	earnings per share
GNP	gross national product
HRM	human resource management
ICT	information and communications technology
IMF	International Monetary Fund
IPO	initial public offering
IOU	I owe you
M & A	mergers and acquisitions
PLC	public limited company
PPP	purchasing power parity
PR	public relations
R & D	research and development
SOE	state owned enterprise
SME	small or medium enterprise
RPI	retail prices index
TQM	total quality management
USP	unique selling point
VC	venture capital
WTO	World Trade Organisation

Depending on the area of study, it is also useful to be familiar with abbreviations for major companies and organisations, e.g. (in the UK):

BT	British Telecom
FSA	Financial Services Authority
NHS	National Health Service
RBS	Royal Bank of Scotland
UCL	University College London

However, writers will also employ more specialised abbreviations in texts, which will be explained in brackets on first use:

> Starting from the resource-based view (RBV) of the firm, it is argued that . . .

> The Technology Readiness Index (TRI) was introduced by Parasuraman (2000).

3 Punctuation

There are many standard abbreviations that have a full stop after them to show that it is a shortened form (*lt.* = litre). Other examples are *govt.* (government), *co.* (company) and *Oct.* (October). With type (b) and (c) abbreviations (see p. 169) there is no standard pattern for using full stops, so both BBC and B.B.C. are used. There is, however, a tendency to use full stops less. The important thing is to employ a consistent style in your work.

4 Duplicate abbreviations

Abbreviations can be confusing. DJ normally stands for 'disc jockey', but in business refers to the Dow Jones Index. GM means General Motors but also 'genetically modified'. LSE may mean the London Stock Exchange or the London School of Economics. It is useful to be aware of these potential confusions. A good dictionary should be used to understand more unusual abbreviations.

5 Abbreviations in writing

Certain abbreviations are found in all types of academic writing. They include:

cf.	compare
e.g.	for example
et al.	and others (used for giving names of multiple authors)
Fig.	figure (for labelling charts and graphs)
ibid.	in the same place (to refer to source mentioned immediately before)
i.e.	that is

K	thousand
NB.	take careful note
op. cit.	in the source mentioned previously
p.a.	yearly (per annum)
pp.	pages
PS	postscript
re.	with reference to

6 Practice exercise: Abbreviations

■ **Explain the abbreviations in the following sentences.**

(a) The failure rate among ICT projects reaches 70 per cent (Smith *et al.*, 2008).

(b) The new laptop's USP was its radical design.

(c) The world's most populous country, i.e. China joined the WTO in 2001.

(d) NB. CVs must be submitted to HR by 30 June.

(e) See the OECD's recent report on the UAE.

(f) The EU hopes to achieve a standard rate of VAT.

(g) The CEO intends to raise spending on R & D by 40 per cent.

(h) Fig. 4. Trade patterns on the www (2003–2008).

(i) BA has opened a new route to HK via KL.

(j) Director of PR required – salary approx. $75K.

(k) Re. the AGM next month: the report is needed asap.

(l) Prof. Wren claimed that the quality of MSc and PhD research was falling.

Academic vocabulary

To read and write academic texts effectively students need to be familiar with the rather formal vocabulary widely used in this area. This unit gives some examples, and provides practice in their use. See also Unit 3.6 Nouns and Adjectives.

1 Basic academic vocabulary

The table on the next page shows examples of some of the more common items.

■ **Use a dictionary to check that you understand them all.**

2 Practice exercise: Academic vocabulary

■ **Choose the most suitable word ending in each case.**

(a) Various economists pred_____ the recession of 2008–9.

(b) A signif_____ number of students have chosen to do that project.

(c) The rate of increase var_____ between 5 per cent and 8 per cent during the 1990s.

Adjective	Noun	Verb
achievable	achievement	achieve
acquired	acquisition	acquire
analytical	analysis	analyse
contributory	contribution/contributor	contribute
creative	creation	create
definitive	definition	define
derived	derivation	derive
distributive	distribution/distributor	distribute
emphatic	emphasis	emphasise
evaluative	evaluation	evaluate
hypothetical	hypothesis	hypothesise
indicative	indication/indicator	indicate
interpretative	interpretation	interpret
invested	investment	invest
predictive	prediction/predictor	predict
reliable	reliability	rely
responsive	response	respond
significant	significance	signify
synthetic	synthesis	synthesise
variable	variation/variable	vary

(d) The first computer was creat_____ during the Second
World War.

(e) Researchers frequently need to ask hypoth_____
questions.

(f) She invest_____ all her capital in the restaurant.

(g) The company puts emph_____ on the reliab_____
of its products.

(h) The essays were evaluat_____ in terms of content and
accuracy.

(i) Stock markets are often indic_____ of forthcoming
changes in the economy.

(j) The cold winter was a contrib_____ factor in the decline
in retail sales.

3 Practice exercise: Academic vocabulary

■ **Complete each sentence with a suitable word from the table in 1.**

(a) Lack of capital was a _____ factor in the company's collapse.

(b) Dividends are _____ to shareholders twice a year.

(c) They received the Nobel Prize for their _____ in economic modelling.

(d) Professor Wagner published the _____ work on energy markets last year.

(e) Over 3,500 questionnaires were _____ in terms of social class.

(f) Three _____ need to be considered when predicting an economic upturn.

4 Academic adjectives

The following adjectives are best understood and learnt as opposites:

absolute	relative
abstract	concrete
logical	illogical
metaphorical	literal
precise	vague *or* approximate *or* rough
rational	irrational
relevant	irrelevant
subjective	objective
theoretical	practical *or* empirical *or* pragmatic

Inflation is an **abstract** concept.

The **metaphorical** use of the word 'key' is probably more common than its **literal** one.

The study of statistics is highly **relevant** to economics.

Her study of women in management was criticised for being too **subjective**.

In Europe, **empirical** research began in the sixteenth century.

5 Practice exercise: Academic vocabulary

■ Complete each sentence with a suitable adjective from the table in 4.

(a) The teacher complained that the quotes were _____ to the title.

(b) His _____ approach led him to ignore some inconvenient facts.

(c) _____ examples are needed to make the argument clear.

(d) It is sufficient to give _____ figures for national populations.

(e) Poverty is usually regarded as a _____ concept.

(f) They approached the task in a _____ way by first analysing the title.

(g) The students preferred examining case studies to _____ discussion.

▶ See Sandra Haywood's website for information about the Academic Word List, with further practice: www.nottingham.ac.uk/~alzsh3/acvocab/.

Articles

Students often find the rules for using articles ('a', 'an' and 'the') confusing. This unit focuses on the definite article, 'the', and provides examples and practice.

1 Using articles

Unless they are uncountable, all nouns need an article when used in the singular. The article can be either **a/an** or **the**. Compare:

(a) **The** Central Bank has reduced the cost of borrowing again;

(b) She went to **a** bank to change some dollars.

In (a) a specific bank is identified.
In (b) the name of the bank is not important.

2 Practice exercise: The definite article

The rules for using **the** (the definite article) are quite complex.

■ **Decide why it is used, or not used, in the following examples.**

(a) The world's largest motor manufacturer is General Motors.

(b) The USA was founded in the eighteenth century.

(c) The government increased regulation of banks in the 1930s.

(d) In many companies, the knowledge of most employees is a wasted resource.

(e) 'The Economist' is published every week.

(f) The south is characterised by poverty and emigration.

(g) John Maynard Keynes, the British economist, died in 1946.

(h) The River Seine runs through the middle of Paris.

(i) The World Bank was founded in 1945.

(j) The euro was introduced in 2002.

3 Use of the definite article

In general, **the** is used with:

(a) superlatives *(largest)*

(b) time periods *(eighteenth century/1930s)*

(c) unique things *(government, world)*

(d) specified things *(knowledge of most employees)*

(e) regular publications *(The Economist)*

(f) regions and rivers *(south/River Seine)*

(g) very well-known people and things *(British economist)*

(h) institutions and bodies *(World Bank)*

(i) positions *(middle)*

(j) currencies *(euro)*

It is **not** used with:

(k) things in general *(banks)*

(l) names of countries, except for the UK, the USA and a few others

(m) abstract nouns, e.g. inflation

(n) companies/things named after people/places, e.g. Sainsbury's, Heathrow airport

4 Practice exercise: Using 'the'

■ In the following sentences, decide if the words and phrases underlined are specific or not, and whether 'the' should be added.

Example:

_____ inflation was the greatest problem for _____ Brazilian government.

Inflation was the greatest problem for **the** Brazilian government.

(a) _____ engineering is the main industry in _____ northern region.

(b) _____ insurance firms have made a record profit in _____ financial year 2008–9.

(c) _____ global warming is partly caused by _____ fossil fuels.

(d) _____ company's CEO has been arrested on_____ fraud charges.

(e) _____ theft is costing _____ banking business millions of pounds a year.

(f) _____ tourism is _____ world's biggest industry.

(g) _____ forests of Scandinavia produce most of _____ Britain's paper.

(h) _____ Thai currency is _____ baht.

(i) _____ computer crime has grown by 200 per cent in _____ last decade.

(j) _____ main causes of _____ industrial revolution are still debated.

(k) Already 3 per cent of _____ working population are employed in _____ call centres.

(l) _____ latest forecast predicts _____ rising unemployment for two years.

(m) Research on _____ housing market is being conducted in _____ business school.

(n) _____ best definition is often _____ simplest.

5 Practice exercise: Articles

■ Complete the following text by inserting a/an/the (or nothing) in each gap. (Note that in some cases more than one answer is possible).

MICROFINANCE

Microfinance is the name given to a system of lending (a) _____ money to poor people in (b) _____ developing countries. Pioneered by Mohammad Yunus of (c) _____ Grameen Bank in (d) _____ Bangladesh, it has been claimed that this process allows 5 per cent of the customers to leave (e) _____ poverty every year, while almost all the clients pay back (f) _____ loans on time. It is, however, quite difficult to research (g) _____ effectiveness of microcredit, because of (h) _____ difficulty of organising a study. Simply comparing borrowers with non-borrowers is unhelpful, since non-borrowers are likely to be less entrepreneurial. But a recent study by (i) _____ two researchers from MIT, (j) _____ American university, in (k) _____ Indian city of Hyderabad, which compared two similar city slums, one with microcredit available and one without, found that (l) _____ process had little significant benefit, with only 20 per cent of loans leading to (m) _____ creation of (n) _____ new businesses.

Caution

The need to avoid absolute statements was mentioned in Unit 2.10 Style. This unit presents more examples of tentative or cautious language, in the form of modal verbs, adverbs and verbs, and practises its use.

1 The use of caution

A cautious style is necessary in many areas of academic writing:

> Primary products **usually** have low supply and demand elasticities.

> **Most** students find writing exam essays difficult.

> Wages **tend to** rise in line with inflation.

Areas where caution is particularly important include:

(a) outlining a hypothesis that needs to be tested, (e.g. in an introduction)

(b) discussing the results of a study, which may not be conclusive

(c) commenting on the work of other writers

(d) making predictions (normally with **may** or **might**)

2 Using modals, adverbs and verbs

Caution is also needed to avoid making statements that are too simplistic:

Marketing is critical to commercial success.

Such statements are rarely completely true. There is usually an exception that needs to be considered. Caution can be shown in several ways:

Marketing **can** be critical to commercial success *(modal verb)*

Marketing is **commonly** critical to commercial success *(adverb)*

Marketing **tends to** be critical to commercial success *(verb)*

■ Complete the table below with more examples.

Modals	Adverbs	Verb/phrase
can	commonly	tends to

3 Practice exercise: Caution

■ Rewrite the following sentences in a more cautious way.

(a) Private companies are more efficient than state-owned businesses.

(b) Workers prefer pay cuts to redundancy.

(c) Older students perform better at university than younger ones.

(d) Word-of-mouth is the best kind of advertising.

(e) English pronunciation is confusing.

(f) Introducing new models of products helps to increase sales.

(g) Global warming will cause the sea level to rise.

(h) Most shopping will be done on the internet in ten years' time.

4 Practice exercise: Caution

Another way to express caution is to use **quite**, **rather** or **fairly** before an adjective.

> a **fairly** accurate summary
>
> **quite** a significant correlation
>
> a **rather** inconvenient location

NB. **quite** is often used before the article. It is generally used positively, while **rather** tends to be used negatively.

■ **Insert quite/rather/fairly in the following to emphasise caution.**

(a) The company's efforts to save energy were successful.

(b) The survey was a comprehensive study of student opinion.

(c) His second book had a hostile reception.

(d) The first year students were fascinated by her lectures.

(e) The decision to invest the pension fund in commercial property was disastrous.

5 Caution in verbs

When referring to sources, the verb used indicates the degree of caution appropriate. Compare:

> Tilic (2004) **states** that the cost of living . . . *(positive)*
>
> Lee (2007) **suggests** that more research is needed . . .
> *(cautious)*

Other verbs that imply tentative or cautious findings are:

> **think / consider / hypothesise / believe / claim / presume**

▶ See Unit 3.14 Verbs of reference

6 Practice exercise: Caution

■ Rewrite the following text in a more cautious style.

6.1   One way to confront the threat of global warming is
          for governments to encourage 'green' industries with
subsidies. By encouraging investment in wind or solar power,
not only will carbon emissions be reduced, but more jobs will
be created. Therefore two problems will be solved at the same
time: unemployment and CO_2 production. It is calculated that
spending on environmental technology will grow by 5 per cent
a year until 2020. By then hundreds of millions of people
worldwide will be working in recycling and carbon-neutral
energy projects, and the danger of global warming will be
significantly reduced.

Linkers

Linkers, which include conjunctions, are words or phrases that join parts of a sentence together, or link a sentence to the next one. It is important to be clear about their meaning for effective reading and writing. This unit describes the different functions of linkers and practises their use.

1 Identifying linkers

■ **Underline the linkers in the following sentences.**

(a) A few inventions, for instance television, have had a major impact on everyday life.

(b) In addition, a large volume of used cars are sold through dealerships.

(c) The definition of motivation is important since it is the cause of some disagreement.

(d) The technology allows consumers a choice, thus increasing their sense of satisfaction.

(e) Four hundred people were interviewed for the survey, then the results were analysed.

(f) However, another body of opinion associates globalisation with unfavourable outcomes.

There are six main types of linker.

■ **Match each of the types below to one of the sentences above.**

(i)   Addition   (b)

(ii) Result   ( )

(iii) Reason   ( )

(iv) Opposition   ( )

(v)   Example   ( )

(vi) Time   ( )

2 Practice exercise: Using linkers

When reading a text, linkers are a kind of signpost to help the reader follow the ideas.

■ **Read the paragraph below and underline the linkers, then decide what their functions are (i.e. types i–vi above).**

2.1   **BIOFUELS**

Newly published research examines some important questions about the growing use of biofuels, such as ethanol made from maize. The production of these has increased sharply recently, but the replacement of food crops with fuel crops has been heavily criticised. Although initially seen as a more environmentally-friendly type of fuel, the research shows that producing some biofuels, for instance biodiesel palm oil, is more polluting than using conventional oil. The ethanol produced from sugar cane, however, can have negative emissions, in other words taking carbon dioxide from the atmosphere instead of adding it. Consequently, it can be seen that the situation is rather confused, and that biofuels are neither a magic solution to the energy problem, nor are they the environmental disaster sometimes suggested.

Linker	Type	Linker	Type
(a) *such as*	*example*	(f)	
(b)		(g)	
(c)		(h)	
(d)		(i)	
(e)		(j)	

3 Practice exercise: Linkers

■ Complete the table with as many examples of linkers as possible.

Addition	Result	Reason	Opposition	Example	Time
Moreover					

4 Practice exercise: Linkers

■ Insert a suitable linker into each gap.

4.1   CHOOSING A BUSINESS SCHOOL

It can be difficult for students to decide whether to attend
business school. The drawbacks, (a) _____ the high
fees and the loss of income, are clear, (b) _____
increasing numbers are applying, (c) _____ the
competition to enter the highest-ranked schools is increasing.
(d) _____ many well-known business people, (e)
_____ Bill Gates, never went to business school,
there is good evidence that an MBA helps students find a well-
paid job more quickly. It can also be hard for students to
choose which school to apply for, (f) _____ there are
so many rankings published, (g) _____ those from
the *Financial Times*, *Business Week* and *The Economist*.
(h) _____ , these tables frequently disagree,
(i) _____ they give different weighting to different
factors. (j) _____ , this lack of agreement may have a
positive aspect, reflecting the diversity of approach found in
the world's great business schools.

---

5 Linkers of opposition

Note the position of the linkers in the following examples:

The economy is strong, **but/yet** there are frequent strikes.

Although/while there are frequent strikes the economy is
strong.

In spite of/despite the frequent strikes the economy is strong.

There are frequent strikes. **However/nevertheless**, the economy is strong.

■ **Write two sentences in each case.**

Example:

The equipment was expensive/unreliable

The equipment was expensive but unreliable.

Although the equipment was expensive it was unreliable.

(a) The government claimed that inflation was falling. The opposition said it was rising.

(i) _____

     _____

(ii) _____

     _____

(b) This department must reduce expenditure. It needs to install new computers.

(i) _____

     _____

(ii) _____

     _____

(c) Sales of the new car were poor. It was heavily advertised.

(i) _____

     _____

(ii) _____

     _____

Nouns and adjectives

It is easy to confuse the noun and adjective form of words such as 'possibility' and 'possible'. This unit gives examples of some of the most common pairs, and provides practice with their use.

1 Using nouns and adjectives

Compare these sentences:

The **efficiency** of the machine depends on the **precision** of its construction.

Precise construction results in an **efficient** machine.

The first sentence uses the nouns 'efficiency' and 'precision'. The second uses adjectives: 'precise' and 'efficient'. Although the meaning is similar the first sentence is more formal. Effective academic writing requires accurate use of both nouns and adjectives.

2 Practice exercise: Nouns and adjectives

■ **Complete the gaps in the table below (p. 191).**

Noun	Adjective	Noun	Adjective
approximation	approximate		particular
superiority		reason	
	strategic		synthetic
politics		economy	
	industrial		cultural
exterior		average	
	high		reliable
heat		strength	
	confident		true
width		probability	
	necessary		long
danger		relevance	

NB. Compare the three nouns:

Economics is a demanding undergraduate degree course *(academic subject)*

The Greek **economy** is heavily in debt *(national economy, countable)*

Economy is needed to reduce the deficit *(saving money, uncountable)*

3 Practice exercise: Nouns and adjectives

■ Insert a suitable noun or adjective from the table in each sentence.

(a) The sales team are _____ the new model
     will sell better.

(b) One _____ of the Swiss economy is its focus
     on banking.

(c) There is a strong _____ that coffee prices
     will fall next year.

(d) The students complained that the lecture was not
     _____ to their course.

(e) The results are so surprising it will be _____
     to repeat the experiment.

(f) The _____ time needed to start a business in
     Italy is 33 days.

(g) Regularly backing up computer files reduces the _____
     of losing vital work.

(h) Revising for exams is a tedious _____ .

(i) These data appear to be _____ and should
     not be trusted.

(j) _____ in the banking system was destroyed
     by years of inflation.

(k) The _____ consequences of the war were
     inflation and unemployment.

(l) They attempted to make a _____ of all the
     different proposals.

4 Practice exercise: Nouns and adjectives

■ Underline the adjective in each sentence and write the related noun in
brackets.

Example:

Several steel producers are <u>likely</u> to shut down next year.
(*likelihood*)

(a) The HR team have just completed a strategic review of pay.

    (_____)

(b) Dr Lee adopted an analytical approach to the inquiry.

    (_____)

(c) Nylon was one of the earliest synthetic fibres.

    (_____)

(d) Her major contribution to the research was her study of privatisation. (_____)

(e) All advertising must respect cultural differences.

    (_____)

(f) Some progress was made in the theoretical area.

    (_____)

(g) A frequent complaint is that too much reading is expected.

    (_____)

(h) We took a more critical approach to marketing theory.

    (_____)

(i) The Department of Social Policy is offering three courses this year. (_____)

(j) Finally, the practical implications of my findings will be examined. (_____)

5 Abstract nouns

A range of nouns is used to express common ideas in academic writing:

Entrepreneurship is an interesting **field.**

The **concept** of class was first discussed in the eighteenth century.

Drucker developed a new **approach** in his second book.

■ **Read the following and find a synonym for each word in bold from the box below.**

(a) The second **factor** in the recession was the loss of confidence.

(b) Smith's **concept** of the division of labour was first presented in 1776.

(c) Snow is a rare **phenomenon** in Rome.

(d) The President's resignation gave a new **aspect** to the national crisis.

(e) A barcode scanner is a **device** used at supermarket checkouts.

(f) Her **field** is the history of life insurance.

(g) The World Bank is a **body** created to support developing countries.

(h) Keynes' work on trade provided new **perspectives** for economists.

(i) Their main **concern** is to prevent a further decline in sales.

(j) The new **system** allows errors to be detected in 12 seconds.

(k) The survey identified three **categories** of employee.

(l) The most serious **issue** raised at the meeting was student accommodation.

process	organisation	machine	theory
event	types	worry	area
views	cause	feature	problem

Prefixes and suffixes

Prefixes and suffixes are the first and last parts of certain words. Understanding the meaning of prefixes and suffixes can help you work out the meaning of a word, and is particularly useful when you meet specialist new vocabulary.

1 How prefixes and suffixes work

'Unsustainable' is an example of a word containing a prefix and suffix. Words like this are much easier to understand if you know how prefixes and suffixes affect word meaning.

Prefixes change or give the meaning.

Suffixes show the meaning or the word class.

Prefix	Meaning	STEM	Suffix	Word class/Meaning
un-	negative	**sustain**	**-able**	adjective/ability

The rate of growth was **unsustainable.** *(i.e. could not be continued)*

2 Prefixes

(a) Negative prefixes: UN-, IN-, MIS- and DIS- often give adjectives and verbs a negative meaning: **un**clear, **in**capable, **mis**hear, **dis**agree

(b) A wide variety of prefixes define meaning, e.g. PRE- usually means 'before', hence **pre**fer, **pre**history and, of course, **pre**fix!

Common prefixes of meaning

■ Find the meaning(s) of each prefix. (NB. some prefixes have more than one meaning.)

auto	autopilot	The plane flew on **autopilot** for six hours.
co	co-ordinator	The **co-ordinator** invited them to a meeting.
ex	ex-president	The **ex-president** gave a lecture on climate change.
ex	exclusive	It is difficult to join such an **exclusive** club.
macro	macroeconomics	Keynes focused on **macroeconomics.**
micro	microscope	She examined the tiny animals with a **microscope.**
multi	multinational	Ford is a **multinational** motor company.
over	overdraft	The bank set their **overdraft** limit at $1 m.
post	postpone	The meeting is **postponed** to next Monday.
re	retrain	The firm **retrained** the staff to use the new software.
sub	subtitle	Chinese films often have **subtitles** in Britain.
under	undergraduate	Most **undergraduate** courses last 3 years.
under	undervalue	Buying **undervalued** assets can be profitable.

3 Practice exercise: Prefixes and suffixes

Prefixes allow new words to be created.

■ **Suggest possible meanings for the recently developed words in bold.**

(a) Criminal activity seems to be very common among the **underclass**.

(b) The passengers found the plane was **overbooked** and had to wait for the next flight.

(c) The **microclimate** in my garden means that I can grow early tomatoes.

(d) It is claimed that computers have created a **post-industrial** economy.

(e) Most CEOs have **ex-directory** phone numbers.

(f) The class was **underwhelmed** by the quality of the lecture.

4 Suffixes

(a) Some suffixes like -ION, -IVE or -LY help the reader find the word class, e.g. noun, verb or adjective.

(b) Other suffixes add to meaning, e.g. -FUL or -LESS after an adjective have a positive or negative effect (thought**ful**/care**less**).

5 Word class suffixes

Nouns	-ER often indicates a person: *teacher, gardener* -EE can show a person who is the subject: *employee, trainee* -ISM and -IST are often used with belief systems and their supporters: *capitalism/capitalist* -NESS converts an adjective into a noun: *sad/ sadness* -ION changes a verb to a noun: *convert/ conversion*

continued . . .

Adjectives	-IVE *effective, constructive* -AL *commercial, agricultural* -OUS *precious, serious*
Verbs	-ISE /-IZE to form verbs from adjectives: *private/ privatise* NB. In the USA only -ize spelling is used, but both forms are accepted in the UK
Adverbs	-LY most (but not all) adverbs have this suffix: *happily*

6 Meaning suffixes

A few suffixes contribute to the meaning of the word:

> -ABLE has the meaning of 'ability': *a **watchable** film, **changeable** weather*

> -WARDS means 'in the direction of': *the ship sailed **northwards***

> -FUL and -LESS: ***hopeful** news, a **leaderless** team*

7 Practice exercise: Prefixes and suffixes

■ Give the word class and suggest possible meanings for:

(a) cancellation

(b) coincidental

(c) uncooperatively

(d) evolutionary

(e) protester

(f) unpredictable

(g) saleable

(h) interviewee

(i) consumerism

(j) symbolically

8 Practice exercise: Prefixes and suffixes

■ Study each sentence and find the meaning of the words underlined.

(a) The film is a French-Italian co-production made by a subsidiary company.

(b) When the car crashed she screamed <u>involuntarily</u> but was <u>unharmed</u>.

(c) Using <u>rechargeable</u> batteries has <u>undoubted</u> benefits for the environment.

(d) The <u>unavailability</u> of the product is due to the <u>exceptional</u> weather.

(e) There is a <u>theoretical</u> possibility of the machine <u>disintegrating</u>.

Prepositions

Prepositions are generally short words such as 'by' or 'at' which are frequently linked to nouns, verbs and adjectives. Their use often seems confusing, but this unit explains how they can be understood. Students should consult a standard English grammar for a full list of prepositional combinations.

1 The main uses of prepositions

■ Underline the prepositions in the following text (ignoring to + infinitives).

> **1.1** The purpose of this paper is to examine the development of the textile industry in Catalonia over the period 1780–1880. This clearly contributed to the region's industrialisation, and was valuable for stimulating exports. In conclusion, the paper sets out to demonstrate the relationship between the decline in agricultural employment and the supply of cheap labour in the factory context.

■ The table lists the main ways of using prepositions. Find one example of each in the text.

Noun + preposition	*purpose of*
Verb + preposition	
Adjective + preposition	
Phrasal verb	
Preposition of place	
Preposition of time	
Phrase	

Note the difference between phrasal verbs and verbs with prepositions:

> The cars are **made in** Korea *(verb + preposition = easy to understand)*

> The researcher **made up** some of his data *(phrasal verb = hard to understand)*

2 Practice exercise: Prepositions

■ Study these further examples of preposition use and decide on their type.

(a) There are a number **of** limitations to be considered . . .
    (noun +)

(b) The results would be applicable **to** all managers . . .
    (_____)

(c) . . . the data was gathered **from** a questionnaire
    (_____)

(d) All the items were placed **within** their categories
    (_____)

(e) The results **of** the investigation are still pertinent . . .

    (_____)

(f) The respondents had spent **on** average 4.9 years . . .

    (_____)

(g) . . . most countries **in** sub-Saharan Africa . . .

    (_____)

(h) . . . **within** a short spell of four years

    (_____)

3 Practice exercise: Prepositions and nouns

■ **Insert a suitable preposition before or after the nouns in the sentences below.**

(a) Evidence is presented in support _____ the value of women's work.

(b) A small change _____ demand can lead to large price rises.

(c) Many examples _____ under-capitalisation were found.

(d) The answer _____ the problem was to retrain the workforce.

(e) Globalisation, _____ an economic sense, describes the opening up of national economies.

(f) The second point is their impact _____ developing countries.

4 Practice exercise: Prepositions in phrases

■ **Complete the following phrases with the correct preposition.**

(a) _____ the whole

(b) point _____ view

(c) in respect _____

(d) _____ spite of

(e) in support _____

(f) _____ the other hand

(g) _____ order to

(h) standard _____ living

5 Practice exercise: Prepositions of place and time

Note the difference between 'among' and 'between':

> **Among** 14 students in the class, only two were from Africa. *(large group)*
>
> He divided his time **between** the offices in Barcelona and Madrid. *(limited number)*

■ **Complete the following sentences with suitable prepositions of place or time.**

(a) _____ the respondents, few had any experience of working abroad.

(b) Industrial production declined gradually _____ 1976 _____ 1985.

(c) Most workers _____ the European Union retire before the age _____ 60.

(d) Adam Smith was born _____ Scotland _____ 1723.

(e) Chocolate sales fall _____ summer and peak _____ Christmas.

(f) _____ the surface, there is no difference _____ male and female responses.

6 Practice exercise: Prepositions

■ **Complete the following text with suitable prepositions.**

This study sets (a) _____ to answer the controversial question (b) _____ whether increased food supply (c) _____ a country makes a significant contribution (d) _____ reducing malnutrition (e) _____ children.

It uses data collected (f) _____ 75 countries (g) _____
1969 and 1987. The findings are that there was a considerable
improvement (h) _____ the majority (i) _____
countries, despite increases in population (j) _____ the
period. However, a clear distinction was found (k) _____
the poorest countries (e.g. (l) _____ South Asia), where
the improvement was greatest, and the wealthier states such
as those (m) _____ North Africa. Other factors, notably
the educational level (n) _____ women, were also found to
be critical (o) _____ improving childhood nutrition.

Punctuation

Accurate punctuation and use of capitals help the reader to understand exactly what the writer meant. While some aspects of punctuation, such as the use of commas, can be a matter of individual style, correct punctuation in areas such as quotation is important.

1 Capitals

It is difficult to give precise rules about the use of capital letters in modern English. However, they should be used in the following cases:

(a)	The first word in a sentence	*In the beginning . . .*
(b)	Names of organisations	*Sheffield Hallam University*
(c)	Days and months	*Friday 21 July*
(d)	Nationality words	*France and the French*
(e)	Names of people/places	*Dr Martin Turner from Edinburgh*
(f)	Book titles (main words only)	*Protectionism and Industrial Decline*

2 Apostrophes (')

Apostrophes are one of the most misused features of English punctuation. They are mainly used in two situations:

(a) To show contractions

He's the leading authority

NB. Contractions are not common in academic English.

(b) With possessives

The professor's secretary *(singular)*

Students' marks *(plural)*

3 Semi-colons (;)

Semi-colons are used to show the link between two connected phrases, when a comma would be too weak and a full stop too strong.

Twenty people were interviewed for the first study; thirty three for the second.

Semi-colons are also used to divide up items in a list when they have a complex structure, as in a multiple citation:

(Maitland, 2006; Rosenor, 1997; *The Economist*, 2006b; University of Michigan, 2000).

NB. Semi-colons are quite rare in many types of writing.

4 Colons (:)

Colons are used:

(a) To introduce explanations

The meeting was postponed: the Dean was ill.

(b) To start a list

Three aspects were identified: financial, social and . . .

(c) To introduce a quotation

As the Duchess of Windsor said: 'You can never be too rich or too thin'.

5 Quotation marks/inverted commas (" "/' ')

(a) Single quotation marks are used to emphasise a word:

The word 'factory' was first used in the seventeenth century.

to give quotations from other writers:

Goodwin's (1977) analysis of habit indicates that, in general, 'it will be more difficult to reverse a trend than to accentuate it'.

to show direct speech:

'Can anyone find the answer?' asked the lecturer.

NB. Longer quotations are usually indented (i.e. have a wider margin) and/or are set in smaller type.

(b) Double quotation marks are used to show quotations inside quotations (nested quotations):

As Kauffman remarked: 'his concept of "internal space" requires close analysis.'

(c) In references, quotation marks are used for the names of articles and chapters, but book or journal titles normally use italics:

Russell, T. (1995) 'A future for coffee?' *Journal of Applied Marketing* 6, 14–17.

6 Others

Hyphens, - , are used with certain words and structures:

> well-engineered/co-operative/three-year-old

Exclamation marks, ! , and question marks, ?

> 'Well!' he shouted, 'Who would believe it?'

Brackets or parentheses, ( ) , can be used to give additional detail:

> Employee attitudes do not affect other dimensions of customer satisfaction (price and quality).

7 Practice exercise: Punctuation

■ **Punctuate the following sentences.**

(a) the study was carried out by christine zhen-wei qiang of the world bank

(b) professor rowans new book the triumph of capitalism is published in new york

(c) as keynes said its better to be roughly right than precisely wrong

(d) three departments law business and economics have had their funding cut

(e) as cammack 1994 points out latin america is creating a new phenomenon democracy without citizens

(f) thousands of new words such as app enter the english language each year

(g) in 2005 frances per capita gdp was 73 per cent of americas

(h) she scored 56 per cent on the main course the previous semester she had achieved 67 per cent

8 Practice exercise: Punctuation

■ **Punctuate the following text.**

8.1 the london school of business is offering three new courses this year economics with psychology introduction to management and ecommerce the first is taught by dr jennifer hillary and runs from october to january the second introduction to management for msc finance students is offered in the second semester and is assessed by coursework only professor wangs course in ecommerce runs in both the autumn and the spring and is for more experienced students

Singular or plural?

The choice of singular or plural can be confusing in various situations, such as in the use of countable and uncountable nouns. This unit illustrates the main areas of difficulty and provides practice with these.

1 Five problem areas

The main problem areas for international students are shown below.

(a) Nouns should agree with verbs, and pronouns with nouns:

Those problems are unique

There **are** many **arguments** in favour

(b) Uncountable nouns and irregular plurals have no final 's':

Most students receive free **tuition**

The main export is tropical **fruit**

(c) General statements normally use the plural:

State **universities** have lower **fees**

(d) 'Each'/'every' are followed by singular noun and verb forms:

> Every **student** receives financial support

(e) Two linked nouns should agree:

> Both the **similarities** and **differences** are important

■ **Find the mistake in the following and decide what type (a–e above) it is.**

(a) The proposal has both advantages and disadvantage.

(_____)

(b) A majority of children in Thailand is vaccinated against measles.   (_____)

(c) There are few young people in rural area.   (_____)

(d) Many places are experiencing an increase in crimes.

(_____)

(e) Each companies have their own policies.   (_____)

2 Group phrases

Study the following 'group' phrases.

singular + plural	plural + singular	plural + uncountable
half the universities	two types of institution	three areas of enquiry
a range of businesses	various kinds of course	several fields of research
one of the elements	many varieties of response	rates of progress

Note that if a verb has more than one subject it must be plural, even if the preceding noun is singular:

> Scores of students, some teachers and the president **are** at the meeting

Their valuable suggestions and hard work **were** vital

Certain 'group' nouns, e.g. team/army/government can be followed by either a singular or plural verb:

The team **was** defeated three times last month *(collectively)*

The team **were** travelling by train and bus *(separately)*

3 Uncountable nouns

(a) Most nouns in English are countable, but the following are generally uncountable, i.e. they are not usually used with numbers or the plural 's'.

accommodation	information	scenery
advice	knowledge	staff
behaviour	money	traffic
commerce	news	travel
data	permission	trouble
education	progress	vocabulary
equipment	research	weather
furniture	rubbish	work

(b) Another group of uncountable nouns is used for materials:

wood / rubber / iron / coffee / paper / water / oil / stone

Little **wood** is used in the construction of motor vehicles

Huge amounts of **paper** are used to produce these magazines

Many of these nouns can be used as countable nouns with a rather different meaning:

Over twenty daily **papers** are published in Delhi

Most **woods** are home to a wide variety of birds

(c) The most difficult group can be used either as countable or uncountable nouns, often with quite different meanings (further examples: business/capital/experience)

> She developed **an interest** in microfinance

> The bank is paying 4 per cent **interest** on six-month deposits

Other nouns with a similar pattern are used for general concepts (love/fear/hope):

> Most people feel that **life** is too short *(in general)*

> Nearly twenty **lives** were lost in the mining accident *(in particular)*

4 Practice exercise: Singular or plural?

■ **In the following sentences, choose the correct alternative.**

(a) Little/Few news about the takeover was released.

(b) He established three successful businesses/business in 1995.

(c) Substantial experiences/experience of report writing are/is required.

(d) It has often been claimed that travel broadens/travels broaden the mind.

(e) Paper was/Papers were very expensive in the twelfth century.

(f) How much advice/many advices were they given before coming to Australia?

(g) She had little interest/few interests outside her work.

(h) The insurance policy excludes the effects of civil war/wars.

(i) Irons were/Iron was first powered by electricity in the twentieth century.

(j) They studied the work/works of three groups of employees over two years.

5 Practice exercise: Singular or plural?

■ **Read the text and choose the correct alternative.**

> **5.1**   A large number of company/companies has/have
> developed website/websites in the last few years.
> Trading using the internet is called e-commerce/e-commerces,
> and this/these is/are divided into two main kinds: B2B and B2C.
> Many business/businesses want to use the internet to sell
> directly to its/their customers (B2C), but large numbers have
> experienced trouble/troubles with security/securities and other
> practical issues. In addition, the high start-up costs and the
> expense/expenses of advertising means/mean that this/these
> company/companies often struggle to make a profit.

Synonyms

Synonyms are different words with a similar meaning. A good writer uses them to avoid repetition and thus provide more interest for the reader. Synonyms are also necessary when paraphrasing or note-making to avoid plagiarism.

1 Using synonyms

■ Underline the synonyms in the following text and complete the table on the following page.

> **1.1** Royal Dutch Shell is the largest oil company in the world by revenue, with a significant share of the global hydrocarbon market. The giant firm employs over 100,000 people internationally, including over 8,000 employees in Britain.

word/phrase	synonym
largest	*giant*
oil	
company	
in the world	
people	

(a) Synonyms are not always exactly the same in meaning, but it is important not to change the register. 'Firm' is a good synonym for 'company', but 'boss' is too informal to use for 'manager'.

(b) The table below shows that although 'enterprise' can be a synonym for 'business', it is not a good synonym for 'corporation'.

a firm	general
a company	general
a business	general
an enterprise	used mainly for new and smaller businesses
a corporation	used with larger companies

(c) Many common words, e.g. culture, economy, or industry have no effective synonyms.

2 Common synonyms in academic writing

■ Study the list of common academic synonyms and check that you understand them.

Nouns		Verbs	
area	field	accelerate	speed up
authority	source	achieve	reach
behaviour	conduct	alter	change
beliefs	ethics	analyse	take apart
benefit	advantage	assist	help
category	type	attach	join
component	part	challenge	question
concept	idea	claim	suggest
controversy	argument	clarify	explain
drawback	disadvantage	concentrate on	focus on
expansion	increase	confine	limit
feeling	emotion	develop	evolve
framework	structure	eliminate	remove
goal	target	evaluate	examine
hypothesis	theory	found	establish
interpretation	explanation	maintain	insist
issue	topic	predict	forecast
method	system	prohibit	ban
option	possibility	quote	cite
quotation	citation	raise	increase
results	findings	reduce	decrease
statistics	figures	respond	reply
study	research	retain	keep
trend	tendency	show	demonstrate
output	production	strengthen	reinforce

3 Practice exercise: Synonyms

■ Find synonyms for the words and phrases underlined.

(a) Professor Hicks <u>questioned</u> the <u>findings</u> of the <u>research</u>.

(b) The <u>statistics show</u> a steady <u>expansion</u> in applications.

(c) The institute's <u>prediction</u> has caused a major <u>controversy</u>.

(d) Cost seems to be the <u>leading drawback</u> to that <u>system</u>.

(e) They will <u>concentrate</u> on the first <u>option</u>.

(f) After the lecture she tried to <u>clarify</u> her <u>concept</u>.

(g) Three <u>issues</u> need to be <u>examined</u>.

(h) The <u>framework</u> can be <u>retained</u> but the <u>goal</u> needs to be <u>altered</u>.

(i) OPEC, the oil producers' cartel, is to <u>cut production</u> to <u>raise</u> global prices.

(j) The <u>trend</u> to smaller families has <u>speeded up</u> in the last decade.

4 Practice exercise: Synonyms

■ Identify the synonyms in this text by underlining them and linking them to the word they are substituting for.

Example: agency – organisation

> 1　The chairman of the UK's food standards **agency** has said that a national advertising campaign is necessary to raise low levels of personal hygiene. The **organisation** is planning a £3m publicity programme to improve British eating habits. A survey has shown that half the population do not wash before eating, and one in five fail to wash before preparing food. There are over 6 million cases of food poisoning in this country every year, and the advertising blitz aims to cut this by 20 per cent. This reduction, the food body believes, could be achieved by regular hand washing prior to meals.

5 Practice exercise: Synonyms

■ In the following text, replace all the words or phrases in bold type with suitable synonyms.

5.1   A leading French company has started a new programme to reduce costs. The **company's programme** aims to **reduce costs** by €100 million per annum. All staff have had pay cuts and work longer every day. The **company aims** to increase profits by 35 per cent next year, and promises that **pay** for all **staff** will be **increased** if that happens.

Time words

Time words such as 'during', 'for' and 'since' are often used in introductions or general statements. The use of some words is restricted to particular tenses. See also Unit 3.15 Verbs – tenses.

1 Using time words

■ **Study the use of the following:**

She went on a training course **for** six weeks.	(with numbers, without start date)
The report must be finished **by** 12 June.	(on or before)
He has been president **since** 2007.	(with present perfect, must specify start date)
They are studying in Bristol **until** March.	(end of a period)
The library was opened two years **ago**.	(usually with past)
The hotel is closed **during** the winter.	(with noun)

Before writing he studied   (often followed by –ing form;
over 100 sources.   also **after)**

He applied in May and was   (often used with numbers; also
accepted two months **later.**   **earlier)**

2 Time words and tenses

■ Compare the tenses used with the following time words and phrases:

Last year there **was** an   (past)
election in Spain.

In the last year there **has**   (present perfect)
been a decline in inflation.

Recently, there **has been**   (present perfect)
a sharp rise in internet use.

Currently, there **is**   (present)
widespread concern
about plagiarism.

3 Practice exercise: Time words

■ Study the schedule for Professor Wang's recent trip and complete the
sentences below with a suitable word. It is now April 16.

March 12	Fly London – Barcelona
March 13–14	Conference in Barcelona
March 15	Train Barcelona – Paris
March 16	Lecture visit to Sorbonne
March 17	Fly Paris – Shanghai
March 18–19	Meeting with colleagues
March 20	Fly Shanghai – London

(a) _____ month Professor Wang made a lengthy trip.

(b) _____ her trip she visited three countries.

(c) _____ March 18th she had travelled 11,000
kilometres.

(d) She was away from home _____ nine days
altogether.

(e) A month _____ she was in Paris.

(f) Two days _____ she was in Shanghai.

(g) She stayed in Shanghai _____ March 20th.

(h) _____ she is writing a report on her trip.

4 Practice exercise: Time words

■ **Choose the best alternative in each case.**

(a) Currently/Recently she has been researching the life cycle of
SMEs in Mumbai.

(b) He worked there until/during the firm went bankrupt.

(c) Dr Hoffman has lived in Cambridge since/for sixteen years.

(d) Last month/In the last month a new book was published on the
business cycle.

(e) Applications must be received by/on November 25th.

(f) Since/During her arrival last May she has reorganised the
department.

(g) During/For the winter most farmers in the region find work in
the towns.

5 Practice exercise: Time words

■ Complete each gap in the following text with a suitable word.

5.1 **EATING OUT**

(a) _____ the last few decades there has been a significant change in eating habits in the UK. (b) _____ the early 1980s eating out in restaurants and cafes has increased steadily. There are several reasons for this trend. Fifty years (c) _____ most women were housewives, and cooked for their families every day. But (d) _____ , with more women working outside the home, less time has been available for food preparation. (e) _____ , 71 per cent of women aged 20–45 are at work, and (f) _____ 2020 it is estimated that this will rise to 85 per cent.

Another factor is the growth in disposable income, which has risen significantly (g) _____ the late 1970s. With more money in their pockets people are more likely to save the trouble of shopping and cooking by visiting their local restaurant.

---

6 Practice exercise: Time words

■ Study the details of Henry Ford's life, and complete the biography below (one word per gap).

1863   Born on a farm near Detroit, USA.

1879   Left home to work as a machinist.

1888   Married Clara Bryant and worked the family farm.

1893   Became Chief Engineer with the Edison company. Began to experiment with petrol engines.

1903   The Ford Motor Company was formed to build the car that he had designed.

1908   The Model T was introduced at a price of $825. It was successful because it was easily maintained and simple to drive.

1909   The price of the Model T was regularly reduced and sales climbed sharply.

1914   Ford shocked the industry by increasing wages to $5 a day. This successfully reduced labour turnover and attracted the best engineers to the company.

1916   The price of the Model T was cut to $360 and sales reached 472,000 annually.

1927   Production of the Model T was finally stopped after selling over 15 million. Sales had been declining for years, and it was replaced by the Model A.

1941   After years of conflict with the labour unions Ford finally recognised the UAW union.

1945   Having kept effective control of the company into his 80s, he allowed his grandson, Henry Ford II, to become president.

1947   Henry Ford died at the age of 83.

6.1   HENRY FORD

Henry Ford was born on a farm near Detroit and lived there (a) _____ he was 16. He returned to the farm nine years (b) _____ to marry Clara Bryant. However, he was more interested in machinery than farming and (c) _____ a few years he became an engineer with the Edison company, working there until 1899. (d) _____ this period he experimented with petrol engines and eventually built a car. (e) _____ 1903 he was confident enough to form a manufacturing company to produce cheap vehicles. The Model T, introduced in 1908, dominated the American market (f) _____ the next twenty years. Ford had been one of the leading American car makers (g) _____ the 1920s, but unions were only recognised in 1941 (h) _____ a long struggle. Henry Ford retained control of his company (i) _____ old age, though (j) _____ his death he allowed his grandson to take over.

Verbs – passives

The passive form is a feature of much academic writing, making it more impersonal and formal, but it is not desirable to use the passive exclusively. This unit provides practice in developing a balanced style.

1 Active and passive

The passive is used when the writer wants to focus on the result, not on the cause:

> **The company** was founded in 1925 by Walter Trimble *(passive)*
>
> **Walter Trimble** founded the company in 1925 *(active)*

In the first sentence, the emphasis is on the company, in the second on Trimble. So the passive is often used in written English when the cause (a person or thing) is less important or unknown.

> Aluminium **was** first **produced** in the nineteenth century *(by someone)*
>
> The currency **was devalued** in the 1930s *(due to something)*

The cause of the action can be shown by adding 'by . . .':

> The banking crisis **was caused by** excessive speculation

The passive is also used in written work to provide a more impersonal style:

> The findings **were evaluated**

NB. All passive structures have two parts:

Form of the verb to be	Past participle
is	constructed
was	developed
will be	re-organised

■ **Change the following into the passive.**

(a) We collected the data and compared the two groups.

(b) I interviewed 120 people in three social classes.

(c) They checked the results and found several errors.

(d) We will make an analysis of the findings.

(e) He asked four managers to give their opinions.

2 Using adverbs

An adverb can be inserted in a passive form to add information:

> This process is **commonly** called 'networking'.

■ **Change the following sentences from active to passive and insert a suitable adverb from the box below.**

Example:

The recession forced half the companies to make redundancies.

Half the companies were **eventually** forced to make redundancies by the recession.

(a) The Connors family ran the company until 1981.

(b) Economists debated the reasons for the Asian currency crisis.

(c) They provided pencils for all students in the exam.

(d) The staff of the advertising agency gave a presentation.

(e) The researchers calculated the percentages to three decimal places.

(f) They called their business the Grand Universal Trading Company.

(g) She researched the life cycles of over 240 companies.

optimistically	helpfully	vigorously	accurately
eventually	vividly	carefully	profitably

3 Practice exercise: Passives

In most texts the active and the passive are mixed.

■ **Read the following article and underline the passive forms.**

3.1 BOOTS THE CHEMIST

When John Boot died at 45, he was worn out by the effort of establishing his herbal medicine business. He had spent his early years as a farm labourer but had worked his way up to be the owner of a substantial business. He was born in 1815, became a member of a Methodist chapel in Nottingham, and later moved to the city. John was concerned by the situation of the poor, who could not afford a doctor, and in 1849 he opened a herbal medicine shop which was called the British and American Botanic Establishment. In the early stages John was helped financially by his father-in-law, while his mother provided herbal knowledge.

On his death in 1860 the business was taken over by his wife, and she was soon assisted by their 10-year-old son, Jesse. He quickly showed the business ability which transformed his father's shop into a national business. Jesse opened more shops in poor districts of the city and pioneered advertising methods. He also insisted on doing business in cash, rather than offering his customers credit.

4 Practice exercise: Passives

■ List the passives in the table below. Decide if the active could be used
instead, and rewrite it if so.

Passive	Active possible?	Active
He was worn out	*Yes*	*The effort ... had worn him out*

■ What would be the effect of using the passive throughout the text?

5 Practice exercise: Passives

The passive is used more in written than in spoken English, but should not be overused, as it can give a very formal tone. In the following text, which continues the history of the Boots company, passives are used throughout.

■ **Change some of them into the active.**

5.1 In 1889 he was introduced to Florence Rowe, the daughter of a bookseller, while on holiday. After they were married the business was affected by her ideas: the product range was enlarged to include stationery and books. The Boots subscription library and in-store cafes were also introduced due to Florence's influence. During the First World War the Boots factories were used to make a variety of products, from sterilisers to gas masks. But after the war Jesse was attacked by arthritis and, worried by the economic prospects, the company was sold to an American rival for £2m. This, however, was made bankrupt during the Depression and Boots was then bought by a British group for £6m, and Jesse's son, John, was made chairman. The famous No.7 cosmetics range was launched in the 1930s and in the Second World War both saccharin and penicillin were produced in the factories. However, recently the company has been threatened by intense competition from supermarkets in its core pharmaceutical business.

Verbs of reference

When introducing quotations or summaries of other writers'
ideas it is necessary to use verbs of reference such as 'claims' or
'states'. These verbs indicate the position of the writer whose
ideas are being summarised. This unit gives examples of common
verbs of reference and practises their use. See also Unit 1.8
References and quotations.

1 Using verbs of reference

Referring verbs are used to summarise another writer's ideas.

> Previn **argued** that the banking crisis was caused primarily by
> lax regulation . . .

> Bakewell (1972) **found** that most managers tended to use
> traditional terms . . .

They may also be used to introduce a quotation.

> . . . as Peter Huber has **observed**: 'Coal itself is yesterday's
> landfill . . .'

2 Common referring verbs

Most of these verbs are followed by a noun clause beginning with 'that'.

(a) The following mean that the writer is presenting a case:

argue   claim   consider   hypothesize   suggest

believe   think   state

Martins (1975) **claimed** that many mergers led to lower profits

(b) A second group describe a reaction to a previously stated position:

accept   admit   agree   deny   doubt

Handlesmith **doubts** Martins' claim that lower profits resulted from . . .

(c) Others include:

assume   conclude   discover   explain   imply

indicate   maintain   presume   reveal   show

Patel (2003) **assumes** that inflation will remain low

3 Practice exercise: Verbs of reference

■ **Write a sentence referring to what the following writers said (more than one verb may be suitable). Use the past tense.**

Example:

Z: 'My research shows that demand for oil is relatively inelastic'.

Z claimed/argued that demand for oil is relatively inelastic.

(a) A: 'I may have made a mistake in my forecast for unemployment'.

_____

_____

(b) B: 'I did not say that women make better managers than men'.

_____

_____

(c) C: 'Small firms are more dynamic than large ones'.

_____

_____

(d) D: 'I support C's views on small firms'.

_____

_____

(e) E: 'I'm not sure, but most people probably work to earn money'.

_____

_____

(f) F: 'After much research, I've found that bonds are the best long-term investment'.

_____

_____

(g) G: 'I think it unlikely that electric cars will replace conventional ones'.

_____

_____

(h) H: 'Somebody should investigate the reasons for employee turnover in call centres'.

_____

_____

(i) I: 'There may be a link between the business cycle and sunspot activity'.

_____

_____

4 Further verbs of reference

A small group of verbs is followed by the pattern (somebody/thing + for + noun/gerund):

> blame   censure   commend   condemn   criticise

NB. All except 'commend' have a negative meaning.

> Lee (1998) **blamed** foreign investors for the panic

A final group is followed by (somebody/thing + as + noun/gerund):

> assess   characterize   classify   define   describe
>
> evaluate   identify   interpret   portray   present
>
> Terry **interprets** rising oil prices as a result of the Asian recovery

5 Practice exercise: Verbs of reference

■ **Rewrite the following statements using verbs from the lists in (4).**

Example:

K: 'X's work is responsible for many of the current economic problems'.

K blamed X's work for many of the current economic problems.

(a) L: 'She was very careless about her research methods'.

(b) M: 'There are four main types of business start-up'.

(c) N: 'That company has an excellent pattern of corporate governance'.

(d) O: 'Their annual results indicate over-reliance on a shrinking market'.

(e) P: 'Only three of the airlines are likely to make a profit this year'.

(f) Q: 'Keynes was the most influential economist of the twentieth century'.

(g) R: 'A bond is a financial instrument giving a fixed return over a limited period'.

(h) S: 'Entrepreneurs need to be hard-working, imaginative risk-takers'.

Verbs – tenses

This unit focuses on the main tenses used in academic writing and explains the way their use is controlled by time words, which were examined in Unit 3.12.

1 Tenses in academic writing

■ Decide which tenses are used in the following examples (verbs in bold) and complete the table on p. 236 to explain why.

(a) According to Hoffman (1996), small firms **respond** more rapidly to change . . .

(b) Currently, inflation in the US **is rising** while imports **are falling**.

(c) Since the summer house prices **have risen** steadily.

(d) In the last three years more students **have been working** part-time.

(e) Two years ago the company **opened** its third hotel.

(f) During the winter **she was studying** international finance.

(g) The report was published in June. It showed that in 2009 profits **had increased** by 55 per cent.

(h) The forecast concludes that interest rates **will peak** next year.

	Tense	Reason for use
a	*Present simple*	*General rule*
b		
c		
d		
e		
f		
g		
h		

2 Practice exercise: Tenses

■ Complete the following sentences by selecting the most suitable
tenses.

(a) Home ownership _____ (rise) steadily since
1950.

(b) AGM _____ (stand for) annual general
meeting.

(c) Last year they _____ (sell) nearly five
million books.

(d) By the time he died in 1987 he _____ (take
    out) over 50 patents.

(e) In ten years most people in the world _____
    (have) a mobile phone.

(f) At the moment the bank _____ (consider) a
    merger proposal from Barclays.

(g) When the market crashed the company _____
    (build) 3 hotels in Asia.

(h) Lee (1965) _____ (dispute) Sakamoto's
    theory.

(i) In the last six years inflation _____ (fall)
    sharply in Europe.

3 Simple or continuous?

(a) In general, the continuous is used to focus on the activity itself or to
    stress its temporary nature. Compare the following:

    She has been writing that report for six days
    (to show duration of temporary activity)

    He is writing an article on probability theory
    (to show temporary nature of activity)

    She writes copy for her advertising agency
    (to demonstrate her normal work)

(b) Also note that certain verbs are rarely used in the continuous. They
    are **state** verbs such as *prefer, own* and *believe.* Another similar group
    is known as **performative** verbs (*assume, deny, promise, refuse, suggest*).

4 Practice exercise: Tenses

■ Select either simple or continuous in each case:

(a) This year the team at Yale _____ (work) on
    a study of microfinance in Indonesia.

(b) He _____ (believe) he will finish the book
    early next year.

(c) This magazine_____ (look for) a writer on business law.

(d) Two years ago she was managing a branch but now she _____ (run) the head office.

(e) The average age of marriage in Italy _____ (rise) by six years between 1970 and 1990.

(f) The company _____ (own) factories in 12 countries.

(g) Most people in the city _____ (live) within two kilometres of their work.

(h) Dr McPherson _____ (attend) a conference in South America this week.

5 Time phrases

When writing paragraphs, it is important to be clear about which time phrases control the tenses of verbs.

■ **Study the following paragraph:**

> **5.1** Recently, the condition of the family **has produced** some of the strongest debate heard in America. The statistics of collapse **have appeared** simple and clear. The proportion of children born outside marriage **rose** from 18 per cent in 1980 to 33 per cent in 1999. The share of households made up of two parents and their children **fell** from 45 per cent in 1960 to only 23 per cent in 2000.

The time phrase *Recently* controls the tense of the first two sentences (present perfect). The next two sentences are in the simple past because of the dates *1980*, *1999*, *1960* and *2000*, which show finished periods:

Time phrase	Verbs controlled
Recently	has produced
	have appeared
1980	rose
1999	fell
1960	
2000	

6 Practice exercise: Tenses

■ Read the text below and select the most suitable tense for each verb in brackets, considering the time phrases in bold.

6.1 **THE BOLOGNA PROCESS**

The first university in Europe was founded in Bologna, Italy, in 1088. **In 1999,** 911 years later, European education ministers (a) _____ (meet) there to plan a common framework for universities in Europe. The aim (b) _____ (be) to standardise the system of studying for degrees to permit students to study in different countries. After 11 years of preparation, **in 2010**, a meeting of 46 ministers in Leuven, Belgium, (c) _____ (agree) the creation of a European higher education area. This (d) _____ (allow) students to take the credits they have gained in one country and transfer them to a degree programme in another.

It seems that many governments **currently** (e) _____ (support) the process as a method of reforming their universities, which (f) _____ (face) strong competition from America. The international league tables continue to be dominated by the 'Ivy League' universities, which (g) _____ (have) much higher incomes than most European institutions. The USA (h) _____ (spend) twice as much of its GDP on higher education than the European average. But **in future** the Bologna process (i) _____ (give) universities more freedom to employ and promote staff, which (j) _____ (make) them more competitive with their transatlantic counterparts. **By 2020** it is hoped that universities in Europe (k) _____ (be) better funded and more independent.

Writing models

Formal letters and emails

Although less common than before electronic communication became available, letters are still important for formal matters, or when an email address is unknown. They are also considered to be more reliable than emails.

However, due to its convenience email is increasingly used for semi-formal as well as informal communication. It is widely seen as a way of having a permanent record of an arrangement or discussion.

1 Letters

■ You have applied for a place on an MA course at a British university. Read the letter you have received in reply on p. 244. Then label the following features of formal letters with the letters (a–l) from the left margin.

Date (*d*)

Ending (____)

Request for response (____)

Greeting (____)

(a)
                    Central Admissions Office
                          Wye House
                          Park Campus
                     University of Mercia
                     Borchester BR3 5HT
                       United Kingdom

(b) Ms J Tan
      54 Sydney Road
      Rowborough RB1 6FD

(c) Ref: MB/373

(d) 3 May 2010

(e) Dear Ms Tan,

(f) **Application for MA Finance**

(g) Further to your recent application, I would like to invite you to the
university for an informal interview on Tuesday 21 May at 11 am. You
will be able to meet the course supervisor, Dr Schmidt, and look round
the Business School.

(h) A map of the campus and instructions for finding the university are
enclosed.

(i) Please let me know if you will be able to attend on the date given.

(j) Yours sincerely,

(k) *M. Bramble*

(l) Mick Bramble
Administrative Assistant
Central Admissions Office

Enc.

Address of recipient   (____)

Address of sender   (____)

Further details   (____)

Reason for writing   (____)

Sender's reference   (____)

Subject headline   (____)

Signature   (____)

Writer's name and job title   (____)

Note the following points:

(a) The example above is addressed to a known individual and the ending is 'Yours sincerely'. However, when writing to somebody whose name you do not know, e.g. The Manager, use *Dear Sir* and *Yours faithfully.*

(b) A formal letter generally uses the family name in the greeting (*Dear Ms Tan*). Certain organisations may, however, use a first name with a family name or even a first name alone (*Dear Jane Tan, Dear Jane*).

(c) If the sender includes a reference it is helpful to quote it in your reply.

2 Practice exercise: Formal letters

■ **Turn the page to write a reply to Mr Bramble making the following points:**

(a) You will attend the interview on the date given.

(b) You would like to have the interview one hour later, due to train times.

54 Sydney Road
Rowborough RB1 6FD

3 Emails

Starting and finishing

The following forms are acceptable ways to begin an email if you know the recipient:

> Hi Sophie, Dear Sophie, Hello Sophie

If you have not met the recipient it may be safer to use:

> Dear Sophie Gratton, Dear Ms Gratton, Dear Dr Gratton

If you need to send an email to a large group (e.g. colleagues) you may use:

> Hi everyone, Hello all

In all cases to close the message you can use:

> Regards, Best wishes, Best regards

You may also add a standard formula before this:

> e.g. Look forward to meeting next week, Let me know if you need further information

The main text

Here you can use common contractions (I've, don't) and idiomatic language, but the normal rules for punctuation should be followed to avoid confusion. Spelling mistakes are just as likely to cause misunderstanding in emails as elsewhere. Always check for spelling and grammar problems before pressing the 'send' key. Note that emails tend to be short, although longer documents may be added as attachments.

4 Practice exercise: Emails

■ Read the following and decide who the sender and recipient might be. Would Rachel expect a reply?

Hello Dr Hoffman,

I'm afraid I can't attend your Accounting Methods class this week, as I have to go for a job interview then. However, I will be there next Tuesday, when I am giving my paper (attached, as requested).

See you then,

Rachel

---

5 Practice exercise: Emails

■ Write suitable emails for the following situations:

(a) You are writing to Mark, a colleague at work, to ask him to suggest a time to meet you tomorrow.

(b) Write to your teacher, Tricia James, to ask her to recommend another book for your current essay.

(c) Write to a group of classmates asking them how they want to celebrate the end of the course.

(d) Write an email in response to the one below. You have never had this book.

According to our records, the copy of *Macroeconomics Today* you borrowed from the library on October 12 is now overdue. Your fine is currently £2.15. Please arrange to return this book as soon as possible.

Tim Carey,
Library Services

Writing CVs

A CV (US resumé) is a summary of your education and work experience used when applying for a job. This unit illustrates the most common format and explains the main points to consider when preparing or updating your own.

1 The contents of a CV

A CV is a personal statement over which you have complete control. When you apply for a job your CV will probably be one of dozens seen by the firm's HR department, so in order to impress it should be as clear, accurate and well-presented as possible. Even if the writers are highly qualified, CVs that contain irrelevant material, are badly organised and include spelling mistakes may well cause the sender to be rejected.

Note the following:

- There is no need to give your gender, date of birth or marital status.

- Two sides is the maximum that most employers want to read.

- Details should be relevant to the particular job you are applying for.

- Avoid clichéd claims such as 'team worker' or 'self starter'.

- Information such as education details is normally presented in reverse chronological order.

- Details of your early education or hobbies are probably irrelevant to the post.

2 Practice exercise: Writing CVs

◼ Study the example CV on P. 251. How could it be improved?

3 Practice exercise: Writing CVs

◼ Write a CV for yourself. When you are satisfied with the format, store it electronically so it can be updated when necessary.

Charles Moreno
31 Cavendish Avenue
London SW3 5GT
07356–723837
cmoreno@swiftserve.net

PROFILE
I am a recent marketing graduate with a background in psychology and some valuable experience of running mixed-media campaigns, looking for a rewarding position that will allow me to build on my knowledge and qualifications.

EDUCATION

Oct 2009-Sep 2010	Mercia Business School, Borchester
	MSc Marketing (modules included Marketing Studies; Operational Marketing; Marketing Contexts)
Sep 2005-Jun 2008	West London University, London
	BSc Psychology (2.1) (Research project in group behaviour)
Sep 2003–Jun 2005	Trent Valley College, Newark
	A-Levels in Psychology, English and German

EMPLOYMENT

Aug 2008–Jul 2009	Voluntary post with 'Help the Homeless' organising fund-raising campaign. Experience with designing leaflets and posters, contacting press and preparing viral marketing strategy.
Jan 2006–May 2007	Part-time post as office assistant with Advantage Market Research, Holland Park, London. General office duties and interviewing.

SKILLS and QUALIFICATIONS
- fluent German speaker
- familiar with most common software, e.g. Excel, MS Office
- clean driving licence

Designing and reporting surveys

Surveys, in which people are asked questions about their behaviour or opinions, are a common feature of academic work. This unit deals with the design of effective questionnaires for surveys, and presents a suitable structure for reporting the results.

1 Conducting surveys

What are the reasons for carrying out surveys?

■ **List your ideas below.**

(a) _____

_____

(b) _____

_____

(c) _____

_____

2 Questionnaire design

(a) Which is the better question?

  (i) How old are you?

  (ii) Are you (a) under 20 (b) between 21 – 30 or (c) over 30?

(b) What is the main difference between the two questions below?

  (i) What do you think of university students?

  (ii) Do you think university students are (a) lazy (b) hardworking
       or (c) average?

(c) How many questions should your questionnaire contain?

When designing your questionnaire:

(a) Limit the number of questions so the respondent can answer them in
    a minute or two. Long and complicated questionnaires will not receive
    accurate replies.

(b) Keep questions clear and simple, and not too personal.

(c) Closed questions (b)(ii) are easier to process, but open questions
    (b)(i) will collect a wider range of responses.

(d) You should try putting the questions to a classmate before beginning
    the full survey, and be ready to modify any that were not clear.

3 Practice exercise: Reporting surveys

■ **Study the report on the following page of a survey carried out on a
  university campus. Complete the report by inserting suitable words
  from the box below into the gaps.**

sample	conducted	slightly	respondents	random	questions
majority	questioned	mentioned	interviewees	common	
	questionnaire	generally	minority		

3.1   STUDENT EXPERIENCE OF PART-TIME WORK

Introduction

With the introduction of course fees and the related increase in student debt, more students are finding it necessary to work part-time. The survey was (a) _____ to find out how this work affects student life and study.

Method

The research was done by asking students selected at (b) _____ on the campus to complete a (c) _____ (see Appendix 1). Fifty students were (d) _____ on Saturday 23 April, with approximately equal numbers of male and female students.

Table 1 Do you have or have you had a part-time job?

	Men	Women	Total	%
Have job now	8	7	15	30
Had job before	4	6	10	20
Never had job	14	11	25	50

Findings

Of the (e) _____ , 30 per cent currently had part-time jobs, 20 per cent had had part-time jobs, but half had never done any work during university semesters (see Table 1). (f)_____ who were working or who had worked were next asked about their reasons for taking the jobs. The most common reason was lack of money (56 per cent), but many students said that they found the work useful experience

cont.   (32 per cent) and others (g) _____ social
benefits (12 per cent).

The 25 students with work experience were next asked
about the effects of the work on their studies. A significant
(h) _____ (64 per cent) claimed that there were
no negative effects at all. However, 24 per cent said that their
academic work suffered (i) _____ , while a small
(j) _____ (12 per cent) reported serious adverse
results, such as tiredness in lectures and falling marks.

Further (k) _____ examined the nature of the
work that the students did. The variety of jobs was surprising,
from van driver to busker, but the most (l) _____
areas were catering and bar work (44 per cent) and secretarial
work (32 per cent). Most students worked between 10 and 15
hours per week, though two (8 per cent) worked over 25 hours.
Rates of pay were (m) _____ near the national
minimum wage, and averaged £6.20 per hour.

The final question invited students to comment on their
experience of part-time work. Many (44 per cent) made the
point that students should be given larger grants so that they
could concentrate on their studies full-time, but others felt that
they gained something from the experience, such as meeting
new people and getting insights into various work
environments. One student said that she had met her current
boyfriend while working in a city centre restaurant.

Conclusions

It is clear that part-time work is now a common aspect of
student life. Many students find jobs at some point in their
studies, but an overwhelming majority (88 per cent) of those
deny that it has a damaging effect on their studies. Most
students work for only 2–3 hours per day on average, and a
significant number claim some positive results from their
employment. Obviously, our survey was limited to a relatively
small (n) _____ by time constraints, and a fuller
study might modify our findings in various ways.

4 Practice exercise: Designing and reporting surveys

Question 1 of the questionnaire is given above Table 1.

■ **What were the other questions in this survey? Using the report, write possible questions below.**

1   *Do you have or have you had a part-time job?*

2   _____

   _____

3   _____

   _____

4   _____

   _____

5   _____

   _____

6   _____

   _____

7   _____

   _____

5 Practice exercise: Designing and reporting surveys

■ What is the main tense in (a) Findings (b) Conclusion? Explain the reasons for the difference.

(a) _____

(b) _____

_____

_____

6 Practice exercise: Designing and reporting surveys

■ You are preparing a survey on one of the following subjects. Write a questionnaire of no more than six questions to collect the most useful data.

(a) Patterns of student spending

(b) Student satisfaction with teaching methods

(c) Customer attitudes to taxi companies

Taking ideas from sources

This unit revises the process of note-making, paraphrasing, summarising and referencing introduced in Units 1.5–1.8, showing how one relevant source can be accurately incorporated into your work.

1 Can money buy happiness?

You have been told to write an essay on the title: 'Can money buy happiness?'.

You have found the following text, which seems relevant to this topic. It is part of an article by A. Penec in a journal called *Applied Econometrics* (volume 44, pages 18–27) published in 2008.

■ Read the text and underline the key points.

1.1   THE MEASUREMENT OF HAPPINESS

Economists have recently begun to pay more attention to studying happiness, instead of just using the more traditional GDP per person. They have found that in the last fifty years there has been no apparent increase in personal happiness in Western nations, despite steadily growing economic wealth. In both Europe and the USA surveys have found no rise in the level of happiness since the 1950s, which seems surprising given that wealthier people generally claim to be happier than poorer people. In America, for example, more than a third of the richest group said they were 'very happy', while only half this proportion of the poorest made the same claim. Although it would be logical to expect that rising national wealth would lead to greater general happiness, this has not happened. Individually, more money does seem to increase happiness, but when the whole society becomes richer, individuals do not appear to feel better off.

One possible explanation has been that people rapidly get used to improvements, and therefore devalue them because they are taken for granted. Central heating is a good example: whereas 50 years ago it was a luxury item, today it is standard in nearly every home. Another theory is that the figures for GDP per person, used to assess national wealth, do not take into account quality of life factors such as environmental damage or levels of stress, which must affect people's feelings of happiness. The report of a commission set up by the French president recently claimed that the French were comparatively better off than had been previously thought, due to their generous holidays and effective health care system, factors which basic GDP figures had ignored.

(a) The text contains five key points:

   (i)   Economists have recently begun to pay more attention to studying happiness, instead of just using the more traditional GDP per person.

   (ii) In the last fifty years there has been no apparent increase in personal happiness in Western nations, despite steadily growing economic wealth.

   (iii) . . . which seems surprising given that wealthier people generally claim to be happier than poorer people.

(iv) One possible explanation has been that people rapidly get used to improvements, and therefore devalue them because they are taken for granted.

(v) Another theory is that the figures for GDP per person, used to assess national wealth, do not take into account quality of life factors such as environmental damage or levels of stress . . .

(b) The next step is to make notes of these points, using paraphrase:

(i) Economists have begun to research happiness, rather than rely on GDP.

(ii) Although W. economies expanded since 1950s, no parallel growth in happiness.

(iii) But more rich people say they are happy than poor.

(iv) Seems that people soon get accustomed to gains, so don't appreciate them.

(v) GDP does not measure environmental or social factors that affect individuals.

(c) These points can now be combined into one paragraph of your essay, using conjunctions where necessary, and including a reference to your source:

> **1.2**   A recent development in economics is the study of personal happiness. Penec (2003) argues that although Western economies have expanded since the 1950s, there has been no parallel growth in happiness. Surveys indicate that rich people generally say they are happier than poor people, but this does not apply to the whole society. One explanation is that people soon become accustomed to gains and so do not appreciate them. It also seems likely that GDP measurement ignores significant social and environmental factors which affect personal well-being.

(d) Continue the same process with the next section of the text by underlining the key points.

1.3   A further explanation for the failure of wealth to increase happiness is the
tendency for people to compare their own position to that of their
neighbours. Studies show that people would prefer to have a lower income, if their
colleagues got less, rather than a higher income while colleagues got more. In other
words, happiness seems to depend on feeling better off than other people, rather
than on any absolute measure of wealth. Further research suggests that having free
time is also closely linked to happiness, so that the pattern of working harder in
order to buy more goods is unlikely to increase well-being. Yet Western societies
generally encourage employees to spend as much time at work as possible.

(e) Make notes on the key points.

(i) _____

_____

(ii) _____

_____

(f) Link the notes together to conclude this section of your essay.

(g) Write a full reference for the source as it would appear in the
list of references.

_____

_____

Writing longer essays

Long essays of 2,500–5,000 words may be required as part of a module assessment. These require more research and organisation than short essays, and this unit provides a model of how such an assignment may be tackled.

1 Planning your work

Longer assignments are normally set many weeks before their deadline, which means that students should have plenty of time to organise their writing.

(a) The first thing is to prepare a schedule for your work. An eight-week schedule might look like the example opposite.

(b) How you actually plan your schedule is up to you, but the important thing is to organise your time effectively. Leaving the writing stage until the last minute will not lead to a good mark, however much research you have done. Although you may be tempted to postpone writing, the sooner you start the sooner you will be able to begin refining your ideas. Remember that late submission of coursework is usually penalised.

Week	Stages of work	Relevant units in *Academic Writing*
1	Study title and make first outline. Look for suitable sources.	1.4
2	Reading and note-making. Keep record of all sources used.	1.2, 1.5, 1.8
3	Reading, note-making, paraphrasing and summarising. Modify outline.	1.2, 1.5, 1.7, 1.8
4	Write draft of main body.	1.10
5	Write draft introduction and conclusion.	1.11
6	Rewrite introduction, main body and conclusion, checking for logical development of ideas and relevance to title.	1.12
7	Organise list of references, contents, list of figures and appendices if required.	1.8, 3.14
8	Proof-read the whole essay before handing it in. Make sure that the overall presentation is clear and accurate.	1.12

(c) Longer essays may include the following features, in this order:

Title page	Apart from the title, this usually shows the student's name and module title and number.
Contents page	This should show the reader the basic organisation of the essay, with page numbers.
List of tables or figures	If the essay includes visual features such as graphs, these need to be listed by title and page number.
Introduction	
Main body	The chief sections of the main body are normally numbered 1, 2, 3 and then subdivided 1.1, 1.2 etc.
Conclusion	
List of references	This is a complete list of all the sources cited in the text. Writers occasionally also include a bibliography, which is a list of sources read but not cited.
Appendices (Singular – appendix)	These sections are for data related to the topic that the reader may want to refer to. Each appendix should have a title and be mentioned in the main body.

2 Practice exercise: Writing longer essays

■ Read the following essay on the topic of motivation. As you read, find examples of the following features:

(a) Three synonyms for 'employees'

(b) A generalisation

(c) A definition

(d) A purpose statement

(e) A quotation and its citation

(f) A passive structure

(g) A phrase showing cause and effect

(h) A paragraph of discussion

(i) An example of tentative or cautious language

2.1   **To what extent are the theories of motivation relevant to modern managers seeking to improve the performance of employees? Illustrate your discussion with a case study from the UK.**

INTRODUCTION

In most contemporary businesses the skills and performance of employees is an essential factor in the success of the enterprise. Clearly, the firm which is most successful in training and motivating its staff is likely to have a significant advantage over its rivals. Not only will it spend less on replacing workers who leave, due to lower labour turnover, but the workforce in general will be more productive and more creative.

Motivation, which has been defined as 'the direction or persistence of action', and describing 'why do people do what they do' (Mullins, 2006:184), can then be distinguished as a key factor for commercial success. It has been the subject of considerable theoretical speculation over the past 70 years, amounting to a substantial body of research. This essay will examine some of the main theories in this field, dividing them into the content theories such as Maslow's and the

continued . . .

cont.   process theories characterised by Vroom's. An attempt will then be made to assess their relevance to the modern workplace, taking as an example the employment policies of Toyota in the UK. This company was chosen due to both the distinctive nature of its labour practices and the fact that, as a Japanese company operating in Britain, it illustrates some of the cross-cultural issues that arise from the globalisation process.

1 MOTIVATION THEORIES

The various theories of motivation are usually divided into content theories and process theories. The former attempt to 'develop an understanding of fundamental human needs' (Cooper *et al.*, 1992: 20). Among the most significant are Maslow's hierarchy of needs theory, McClellan's achievement theory and Herzberg's two factor theory. The process theories deal with the actual methods of motivating workers, and include the work of Vroom, Locke and Adams.

1.1 Content theories

Maslow's hierarchy of needs theory was first published in 1943 and envisages a pyramid of needs on five levels, each of which has to be satisfied before moving up to the next level. The first level is physiological needs such as food and drink, followed by security, love, esteem and self-fulfillment (Rollinson, 2005:195–6). This theory was later revised by Alderfer, who reduced the needs to three: existence, relatedness and growth, and re-named it the ERG theory. In addition, he suggested that all three needs should be addressed simultaneously (Steers *et al.*, 2004: 381). McClelland had a slightly different emphasis when he argued that individuals were primarily motivated by three principal needs: for achievement, affiliation and power (Mullins, 2006: 199).

In contrast Herzberg suggested, on the basis of multiple interviews with engineers and accountants during the 1950s, a two-factor theory: that job satisfaction and dissatisfaction had differing roots. He claimed that so-called hygiene factors such as conditions and pay were likely to cause negative attitudes if inadequate, while positive attitudes came from the nature of the job itself. In other words, workers were satisfied if they found their work intrinsically interesting, but would not be motivated to work harder merely by good salaries or holiday allowances. Instead workers needed to be given more responsibility, more authority or more challenging tasks to perform (Vroom and Deci, 1992: 252). Herzberg's work has probably been the most influential of all the theories in this field, and is still widely

continued . . .

cont.   used today, despite being the subject of some criticism, which will be considered later.

1.2 Process theories

Vroom's expectancy theory hypothesises a link between effort, performance and motivation. It is based on the idea that an employee believes that increased effort will result in improved performance. This requires a belief that the individual will be supported by the organisation in terms of training and resources (Mullins, 2006). In contrast, Locke emphasised the importance of setting clear targets to improve worker performance in his goal theory. Setting challenging but realistic goals is necessary for increasing employee motivation: 'goal specificity, goal difficulty and goal commitment each served to enhance task performance' (Steers, 2004: 382). This theory has implications for the design and conduct of staff appraisal systems and for management by objective methods focusing on the achievement of agreed performance targets.

Another approach was developed by Adams in his theory of equity, based on the concept that people value fairness. He argued that employees appreciate being treated in a transparently equitable manner in comparison with other workers doing similar functions, and respond positively if this is made apparent (Mullins, 2006). This approach takes a wider view of the workplace situation than some other theories, and stresses the balance each worker calculates between 'inputs', i.e. the effort made, and 'outputs', which are the rewards obtained.

1.3 Theory and practice

It should be emphasised that these various approaches are by no means mutually exclusive, and to some extent merely reflect alternative viewpoints. For instance, various similarities have been noted between the theories of Maslow and Herzberg. As Rollison (2005: 205) points out, Herzberg's hygiene factors roughly correspond to Maslow's physiological, safety and affiliation needs, and Herzberg's motivators are similarly equivalent to Maslow's esteem and self-actualisation needs. But both have been criticised as being too general; ignoring individual personality differences in favour of a simplistic overall scheme. In this respect the process theories accommodate better to the variations between different employees.

A further objection is that Herzberg based his work on interviews with accountants and engineers, both professional classes, and that their attitudes may not apply to

continued . . .

cont.   manual or less-skilled workers. In some cases researchers have failed to replicate Herzberg's results, and it has been argued that the two factors are not as distinct as he proposed, but can overlap in some people. In addition, critics have pointed out that it is common to blame dissatisfaction at work on externals such as working conditions (hygiene factors), while people are generally pleased to take credit for their own work (motivators). As both Maslow and Herzberg did their research over 50 years ago, it is further argued that they reflect an outdated view of work with limited relevance to modern practices.

2 A CASE STUDY – TOYOTA UK

Toyota, the Japanese motor manufacturer, opened its first European production facility in the UK in 1989. This company claims to have high standards of employment practice to maximise the productivity of its workforce, and has come in some ways to represent the Japanese model of paternalistic employer. According to its statement of general principles:

> We also recognise that people are the foundation of the Company and that highly competent, motivated and respected Members commit to work toward fulfilling the objectives of the Company. We strive to provide to the individual both growth opportunity and stable employment through the achievement of the long-term prosperity of the Company. (Toyota UK, 2010)

The company claims to improve its employees' (always referred to as 'members') job satisfaction by operating a job rotation plan. They are given the responsibility for the quality of their own part in the production process. The safety and welfare of the staff is also highlighted by Toyota, who provide medical insurance and comprehensive safety training. They also operate a scheme to obtain regular feedback from workers, to assist management in their understanding of employees' opinions.

In many ways Toyota's approach seems to conform closely to the Maslow/ Herzberg model. Physiological needs are met by providing good levels of pay, while safety needs are addressed by the medical insurance and safety training. The emphasis on good communication and providing fair and equitable treatment for all achieves the social need, and performance appraisals and the delegation of authority meets the requirements for self-esteem. Finally, the system of job rotation and continuous product development should allow workers to use their creativity.

continued . . .

cont. Despite this, two issues at Toyota need consideration. Firstly the company employs both Japanese and British workers in its UK plant. It is possible that working practices devised in its home country, Japan, may not always be suitable for application to other cultures, and may need to be modified to motivate adequately British workers who may, for example, place more value on holidays than their Japanese counterparts. For their part, the expatriate Japanese workers in the UK are likely to have very distinct needs, particularly with regard to their families, as a result of living outside their own culture.

Another issue is the difference in work attitudes between professionals such as engineers and assembly line workers. While the former, who were the subject of Herzberg's original research, may put more value on work satisfaction, the latter may be more concerned with factors such as the speed of the assembly line. Despite the company's insistence of equal treatment for all, in practice this may be difficult to achieve.

CONCLUSION

Although the main theories of motivation such as Herzberg's and Maslow's have been in circulation for some time they still have relevance to the modern workplace. While possibly offering an over-simplified approach, their basic principle of a series of employee needs, which must be addressed in order to achieve motivation, is a useful basis for study. However, no over-arching theory is likely to reflect the full complexity of the contemporary employee-employer relationship, especially in the current uncertain economic climate.

The process theories of Vroom, Locke and Adams may prove more useful in dealing with the contemporary scene, with their focus on trust, goal setting and fairness. Clearly, these do not exclude the content theories, as can be seen in the example of Toyota, where the strong emphasis on respecting and valuing all workers equally is matched by provision for the hierarchy of needs. This case also acts as a reminder that the modern multi-cultural workforce may well not all share the same values, thereby adding another layer of complexity to the task of the management. One promising field for further research might be to compare the motivation of professional workers in a firm such as Toyota with that of the blue-collar employees, in order to test how far the theories of Herzberg and Maslow are generally applicable.

Answers

Providing answers for a writing course is less clear cut than for other language areas. In some exercises there is only one possible answer, but in other cases several possibilities exist. Teachers need to use common sense, and accept any reasonable answer. In the case of exercises where students can choose their own topic and it is therefore impossible to provide an answer, students still appreciate having a model answer, and so some have been included.

ANSWERS: ACADEMIC WRITING QUIZ

1. b (see Unit 1.2)
2. c (see Unit 1.1)
3. a (see Unit 1.4)
4. c (see Unit 1.11)
5. b (see Unit 1.3)
6. c (see Unit 1.5)
7. a (see Unit 1.8)
8. b (see Unit 1.6)
9. c (see Unit 1.10)
10. a (see Unit 1.11)
11. b (see Unit 1.12)
12. c (see Unit 1.2)

ANSWERS: PART 1

1.1 Background to writing

1 What is academic writing?

Possibilities include:

- semi-formal vocabulary, lack of idioms
- use of citation/references
- normally impersonal style
- use of both passive and active

2 Common types of academic writing

Notes – A written record of the main points of a text or lecture, for a student's personal use.

Report – A description of something a student has done, e.g. conducting a survey.

Project – A piece of research, either individual or group work, with the topic chosen by the student(s).

Essay – The most common type of written work, with the title given by the teacher, normally 1000–5000 words.

Dissertation/Thesis – The longest piece of writing normally done by a student (20,000+ words) often for a higher degree, on a topic chosen by the student.

3 The structure of academic texts

(a) abstract
(b) references
(c) appendix

(d) acknowledgements
(e) literature review
(f) case study

4 The format of academic writing

(a) title
(b) sub-title
(c) heading
(d) phrase
(e) sentence
(f) paragraph

6 Simple and complex sentences

Model sentences:

(a) In 2007 the company produced nearly 165,000 vehicles.
(b) Vehicle production fell in 2008.
(c) In 2009 fewer vehicles were made than in the four previous years.
(d) Between 2005 and 2009 vehicle production peaked in 2007, when the number reached
     164,000.

7 Writing in paragraphs

▶ **See 1.10. Organising paragraphs 1**

para 2 begins: The first issue to . . .
para 3 begins: Diversification must also . . .
para 4 begins: A further consideration . . .

1.2 Critical reading

1 Academic texts

Text 1 – Yes – this appears to be an academic article
Text 2 – No – apparently an informal personal report
Text 3 – Possibly – appears to be a newspaper article
Text 4 – Yes – apparently an academic article

Possible answers:

Feature	Example
1 Formal vocabulary	The marketing planning process in tourism marketing . . . the extent of political-economic dependency . . .
2 Use of references	(Buckley and Witt, 1990; Hall, 1991)
3 Impersonal style	. . . it has also long been recognised that. . .
	. . . it is important to study the tourists' attitude.

4   Long, complex sentences   Equally, from a political perspective, the nature of state
                                    involvement in and policies for tourism is dependent on both
                                    the political-economic structures and the prevailing political
                                    ideology in the destination state, with comparisons typically
                                    made between market-led and centrally planned economies.

2 Types of text

Possible answers:

Text type	Advantage	Disadvantage
1 Textbook	Written for students	May be out of date
2 Website	Usually up-to-date	Possibly unreliable
3 Journal article	Often focuses on a special area	May be too specialised or complex
4 Official report (from government)	Contains a lot of detail	May not be objective
5 Newspaper or magazine article	Easy to read and up-to-date	May not be objective and not give sources
6 e-books	Easily accessible	Must be read on screen

4 Using library catalogues

Title 1 is up-to-date and appears to be a general introduction. The other titles are more specialised, but title 2 is also recent and might contain some relevant sections.

6 Reading methods

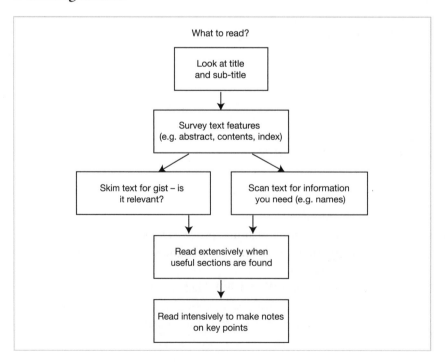

Possible answers:

(a) skimming is to find the main ideas
    scanning aims to locate specific details
(b) text genre recognition
    dealing with new vocabulary

8 Assessing texts critically

(b) 1   Probably unreliable. The adjectives used (easily, quickly) and the lack of concrete
        information show that this text is not to be trusted.
    2   Probably reliable. The advice the writer is giving appears commonsense, although not
        everyone might agree with all of it (e.g. cooking is fun).
    3   Probably reliable. The facts given can be confirmed by students' own experience.

(c) *Change on the farm*

    Pro: Current, relevant, some statistics
    Con: Lack of detail, no references, rather superficial

9 Critical thinking

The responses to these questions will vary from student to student, which is the nature of the
critical approach.

1.3 Avoiding plagiarism

2 Degrees of plagiarism

(1) Y   (2) Y   (3) Y   (4) N   (5) Y

(6) N   (7) Y   (8) N   (9) Y/N   (10) Y

3 Summarising and paraphrasing

(a) acceptable – a correctly referenced summary
(b) plagiarised – original wording with minor changes to word order
(c) acceptable – a correctly referenced quotation
(d) technically plagiarism – mistake in date means the citation is incorrect
(e) plagiarised – some original wording and no citation

1.4 From understanding titles to planning

2 Essay titles

(a) How/why/what
    Asking for a description of the process of and reasons for segmentation, and analysis of the
    social and economic forces involved.
(b) Critically evaluate
    Asking for an examination of the impact of the internet on the standard theories of
    internationalisation.

(c) Describe/critically examine

Asking for an account of the problems faced by HRM in this area and an evaluation of how some companies deal with this.

(d) Discuss/Consider

Asking for an evaluation of some of the literature on these topics, and the impact these theories might have on management.

3 *Practice exercise: Essay titles*

 (1) Break down into the various parts and their relationships
 (2) Decide the worth or value of a subject
 (3) Give a detailed account of something
 (4) Look at various aspects of a topic, compare benefits and drawbacks
 (5) Divide into sections and discuss each critically/consider widely
 (6) Give examples
 (7) Give a simple, basic account of the main points of a topic
 (8) Explain a topic briefly and clearly
 (9) Make a proposal and support it
(10) Deal with a complex topic by reducing it to the main elements

5 *Essay length*

NB. These figures are only a guide and individual students may have a different approach.

(a) Describe/How
    Approximately 50:50
(b) Explain/Discuss
    Approximately 30:70
(c) What/Discuss
    Approximately 50:50

6 *Outlines*

(c) Lists are more logical, make it easier to allocate space, but are rather inflexible.
    Mind maps are more flexible as extra items can be added easily.
(d) Possible outline:
    <u>Reducing harmful impacts</u>
    (i)   Limit numbers of visitors
    (ii)   Keep visitors in limited area
    (iii) Control new developments carefully
    (iv)   Provide new infrastructure, e.g. roads of value to all
    (v)   Give locals opportunity to start new businesses

1.5 Finding key points and note-making

1 *Note-making*

(a) to prepare for essay writing
(b) to avoid plagiarism

(c) to keep a record of reading/lectures

(d) to revise for exams

(e) to help remember main points

2 Note-making methods

The notes are paraphrased, not copied from the text.

3 Practice exercise: Finding key points

Possible titles:

> Marketing to the older generation
> Selling to retired people
> An ageing market

Key points:

(a) The generation born after the Second World War, sometimes called the baby-boomers, are now reaching retirement age, and businesses are starting to realise that they are a wealthier market than any previous retirement group.

(b) There are, however, certain difficulties in selling to this market. Some customers resent being addressed as 'old' since they see themselves as more youthful, while there is a huge variation in the profile of the baby-boomers.

4 Relevance

Key points:

1 The practice of imposing taxes on products that are thought to have a negative social impact, such as alcohol, has been accepted for several hundred years . . .

2 It has recently been suggested in the USA that so-called junk food should be taxed in order to compensate for the social costs of the obesity it is believed to cause. This proposal is based on the estimate of the medical costs of obesity, which is thought to be linked to cancer, diabetes and heart disease.

3 A study of the long-term effects of changes in food prices (Goldman, Lakdawalla and Zheng, 2009) argues that significant changes in consumption, and hence obesity levels, can be achieved over the long-term.

4 But the link between junk food and ill-health is not easily determined. A physically active person could eat hamburgers daily and still keep slim.

5 It has even been suggested that such a 'fat tax' might have the opposite effect and reduce activity levels by forcing people to spend more time preparing food for themselves, instead of buying it from fast-food outlets (Yaniv, Rosin and Tobol, 2009).

6 . . . other studies on the effects of alcohol and tobacco taxes indicate that the heaviest users of these products are the least influenced by price rises, . . .

6 Practice exercise: Note-making

Source: Rohan, J. (2010) Public Health Review 8 p. 36

Taxing junk food

(1) Goods > social harm e.g. alcohol have been taxed since 18th C.
(2) US proposal to tax junk food – reduce obesity (medical costs – diabetes, heart disease)
(3) Goldman, Lakdawalla and Zheng, 2009 claim that raising food prices can reduce consumption in long term
(4) No clear link health/junk food – active people stay thin
(5) Yaniv, Rosin and Tobol, 2009 argue that tax on fast food might have undesired effect of making people cook more > cut their exercise time
(6) Research on tax on alcohol shows that main users are unaffected by increase in prices

7 Practice exercise: Finding key points and note-making

Source: Caballero J. and Poledna Z. (2010) *European Business Prospects*, London: University Press, p. 351

Predatory pricing (PP) = using size to lower prices below cost to harm competitors
• In US 1890 Sherman Antitrust Act example of govt. attempt to control monopolies
But low prices benefit customers + predation hard to prove legally
• good reasons for selling below cost, e.g. new product promotion
• bundling (selling several items together) makes proof harder (i.e. calculating individual profit margins)
Example:
5/09 EU fined Intel €1 bn. for PP against rival AMD – but very complex case and Intel appealed verdict

1.6 Paraphrasing

2 Practice exercise: Paraphrasing

a   Quite good, but lack of precision (at that time) and unsuitable register (bosses)
b   The best paraphrase, with all main points included and a significantly different structure.
c   A poor paraphrase, with only a few words changed and extra and inaccurate information added (Britain was the only country . . .)

5 Practice exercise: Synonyms

A number of possibilities are acceptable here. These are suggestions.

(b) It started in France and Germany, but accelerated in the United States.
(c) There Henry Ford modified the moving assembly line from the Chicago meat industry to car manufacturing, thereby inventing mass production.

6 Practice exercise: Word class

(b) After the Second World War the focus of car makers was on the style of their products, to encourage more frequent model changes.
(c) From the 1970s the industry was criticised for its inefficient vehicles which wasted petrol.

7 Practice exercise: Word order

(b) Some of the most famous brands in the world are today owned by the industry.

(c) Currently, saturated markets and increased competition threaten many car makers.

8 Practice exercise: Paraphrasing

Model paraphrase:

> The expansion of contemporary capitalism matches the rise of the automobile industry. After starting in Germany and France, it accelerated in the United States. There the moving assembly line was modified by Henry Ford from the Chicago meat industry to manufacturing cars; thereby inventing mass production. General Motors dominated the world's car companies in the 1920s, with help from the managerial theories of Alfred Sloan. After the Second World War the focus of car makers was on the style of their products, to encourage more frequent model changes. From the 1970s the industry was criticised for its inefficient vehicles which wasted petrol. At this time increasingly militant trades unions defended their members' jobs. Some of the most famous brands in the world are today owned by the industry, although currently saturated markets and increased competition threaten many car makers.

9 Practice exercise: Paraphrasing

Model paraphrase:

> Government investment in low-emission energy schemes is frequently proposed as a method of creating jobs. Such jobs appear to cut national dependence on oil imports while additionally reducing the production of carbon dioxide. In the USA it is estimated that $100 billion spent by the state would lead to two million new jobs, and already several countries, e.g. Indonesia, Germany and Spain, have begun investing in green technology.

> But it is argued that this government expenditure does not always have positive results, since spending on other technologies might also create work, while higher government spending is likely to inflate the cost of borrowing. Giving subsidies to (relatively inefficient) renewable energy also tends to increase the cost of electricity.

> A Spanish researcher has examined the cost of the government's subsidy of €29 billion for low-carbon energy. Although this will create 50,000 jobs over 25 years, they are likely to cost twice as much as jobs that might have been created by private firms, if they had spent the same money. While these calculations ignore the positive effects of reducing the consumption of non-renewables, they demonstrate that green subsidies do not necessarily have clear-cut advantages.

1.7 Summarising

1 Summarising

A good summary: selection of most important aspects/clear description/accuracy

2 Stages of summarising

(Other answers possible)

(a) difficult
(b) Select
(c) notes
(d) summary
(e) readable

3 Practice exercise: Summarising

1 = c
2 = b
3 = a

5 Practice exercise: Summarising

(Includes answers for 4.)

Model answers:

(a) Falling levels of fertility have generally been found as countries become richer.
(b) In some, number of children born fell below replacement rate.
(c) Two results: smaller populations and larger numbers of elderly needing assistance.
(d) Recent research claims that a new situation may be developing.
(e) Comparison of HDI (human development index: life expectancy, income and education) with fertility found that in most highly rated (+0.9) countries, fertility is rising.

6 Practice exercise: Summarising

Model summary:

Falling levels of fertility have generally been found as countries become richer. In some, the number of children born has fallen below the replacement rate. There are two likely results: smaller populations and larger numbers of elderly needing assistance. But recent research claims that this pattern may be changing. A comparison of HDI (human development index: life expectancy, income and education) with fertility found that in most highly rated (HDI +0.9) countries, fertility is rising.

7 Practice exercise: Summarising

Model summary:

Research suggests that the long-term decline in human fertility may be reversing in some of the most advanced societies.

8 Practice exercise: Summarising

Model summary:

The Washlet is an expensive lavatory which is popular in Japan, with a range of special features. Its maker, the Toto company, is hoping to develop sales in the West, but different regulations about toilet design and electrical fittings make this a challenging goal.

1.8 References and quotations

1 Referring to sources

The first is a summary and the second is a quotation. A summary is more flexible, while a quotation uses the authentic language of the original.

2 Practice exercise: References

(a) N   (b) Y   (c) Y   (d) N   (e) Y   (f) N

5 Examples

Model answers:

(a) According to Hoffman (2009) mobile phones have a powerful impact in the developing world as they offer previously unavailable services, and have led to the growth of new, focused local operators.

(b) Hoffman points out that the special conditions in the developing world have produced new phone operators: 'that are larger and more flexible than Western companies, and which have grown by catering for poorer customers . . .' (Hoffman 2009: 87).

(c) Hoffman (2009) argues that the impact of mobile telephony on developing countries is significant as they offer services previously unavailable, and has led to the growth of new local operators which: 'are larger and more flexible than Western companies, and which have grown by catering for poorer customers . . .' (Hoffman 2009: 87).

7 Organising the list of references

(a) (i)   Cable
    (ii)   Brander and Spencer/Conrad
    (iii)   Intriligator
    (iv)   Gribben
    (v)   *The Economist*
    (vi)   OECD
(b) (i)   author/date/title/place of publication/publisher
    (ii)   author(s)/date/article title/journal title/volume number/page numbers
    (iii)   author/date/chapter title/editors/book title/place of publication/publisher
    (iv)   author/date/title of article/URL of article/date of access
    (v)   magazine title/URL of article/access date or date of issue
    (vi)   name of organisation/date/title/place of publication
(c) for book and journal titles
(d) for titles of books (not articles)
(e) under the title of the publication
(f) (i)   Brander and Spencer, 1985
    (ii)   Cable, 1983
    (iii)   Conrad, 1989
    (iv)   Gribben, 2009

(v)   Intriligator, 2005
(vi) OECD, 1998
(vii) *The Economist*, 2009

1.9 Combining sources

1 Mentioning sources

(a) 6
(b) Level of technology anxiety
(c) Venkatesh
(d) Mick and Fournier
(e) 2

2 Practice exercise: Sources

(a) Possible answer:

Summary	**Original**
globalisation, although not a modern phenomenon . . .	globalisation is not a new phenomenon, but has its roots in the age of colonial development in the seventeenth and eighteenth centuries

(b) argues, emphasises, highlights
(c) However
(d) In contrast, Conversely

3 Practice exercise: Combining sources

Model answer:

> Lin (2006) demonstrates that by allowing companies to transfer production easily from high-wage to low-wage countries, globalisation benefits both the multi-nationals and the workers who gain employment, while disadvantaging those where the facility has been lost. She also mentions the plight of the poorest nations, which have gained little from globalisation. Costa (2008) points out that the significant growth in international trade since 1990 has assisted many developing economies, such as the BRIC group. Brokaw (2002) examines the varying strategies of multi-nationals, which he claims have won substantial advantages from trade liberalisation.

1.10 Organising paragraphs

2 Practice exercise: Paragraphs

(a) Topic sentence
    Example
    Reason
    Argument 1
    Argument 2
    Argument 3

(b) for example/It is widely believed/In addition/But above all
(c) Despite this

3 Development of ideas

(a) Topic sentence   iv
    Definition   ii
    Result 1   i
    Result 2   vi
    Result 3   v
    Conclusion   iii

(b) All these claims
(c) These/but/When this/Others/in other words/Even

5 Practice exercise: Organising paragraphs

Model answer:

(a)

1	Topic	It has been argued that rises in the rate of home ownership can increase the rate of unemployment.
2	Reason	This is because home ownership appears to make people more reluctant to move in order to find work.
3	Example	Spain is an example of a country where high rates of home ownership coincide with high unemployment, while Switzerland demonstrates the opposite.
4	Argument	This theory, however, remains controversial.
5	Conclusion	It is clear that other factors, such as the liquidity of the housing market, must play a role in the relationship.

(b)

1   The theory was lent support by the performance of the housing market in such US states as California and Florida during the recession 2008–9.
2   These states had all experienced a major housing boom during the 1990s.
3   But after the start of the recession the rate of house moving declined steeply.
4   It appears that one factor in this slowdown was the number of households in negative equity.
5   Having negative equity means that a house would be sold at a loss.
6   Therefore the recession may be deepened if labour becomes more static, as a result of high home ownership rates.

1.11 Introductions and conclusions

1 Introduction contents

(a) • a definition of any difficult words in the title
   • a review of some of the literature on the subject
   • your purpose in writing this paper
   • your research method and results
   • some background to the topic, showing the relevance of your work
   • an outline of your structure
   • the limitations of the paper
(b) (i)   purpose
   (ii)   method
   (iii) definition
   (iv)   limitation
   (v)   outline
   (vi)   background
   (vii) literature review

2 Introduction structure

Essential: A review of some literature/Your purpose/Your method/Background/Outline
Optional: Definitions/Limitations

3 Opening sentences

Model answers:

(a) In recent years there has been a steady criticism of the lack of women in senior management.
(b) The spectacular growth in international tourism in the last forty years has been caused by several significant 'pull' factors.
(c) In the last 20 years most Western economies have seen a steady decrease in inflation rates.
(d) Monopoly industries were a feature of the command economies of the communist bloc countries such as Czechoslovakia before 1990.

4 Practice exercise: Introductions

Sample introduction:

State control can be defined as meaning that industries are publicly financed, usually with ultimate control exercised by government ministers. Over the last two decades there has been a global tendency to privatise many key industries which had formerly been in public ownership such as electricity and gas supply, railways and iron and steel production. There is continuing debate as to how far this process can continue; for example some countries have privatised railways while in others they remain under state control.

This paper aims to evaluate the benefits and drawbacks of state control of industry. Using examples from the UK and France between 1990 and 2005, a comparison will be made of two key industries: electricity and railways. The first section will examine the benefits obtained from public ownership, then the disadvantages will be analysed. The final section will attempt to assess the limits of the privatisation process.

5 *Conclusions*

(a) Y (b) Y (c) N (d) Y (e) Y (f) Y (g) Y (h) N

(i) f (ii) b (iii) e (iv) d (v) g (vi) a

6 *Practice exercise: Conclusions*

Model conclusion:

> It has been shown that, although in some situations a strong economy is linked to low rates of home ownership, this is not always the case. There have been claims that owning a house may make people reluctant to move in order to find work, and this theory seems to be supported by the examples in some US states during the recession of 2008–9. However, it appears that the main factor here was negative equity, rather than just ownership. As negative equity is the product of a house price bubble, it seems that the principal threat to a national economy is rapid inflation of house prices to unsustainable levels.

> Consequently, it can be suggested that governments should take steps to control the expansion of credit to prevent housing bubbles by discouraging risky lending. Clearly, this short essay has only outlined the main features of this topic and many aspects would benefit from more study. One possible field for further research would be to investigate the reasons why some home owners default on their mortgage payments.

1.12 Rewriting and proof-reading

2 *Practice exercise: Rewriting*

(a) Rather short (100 words) for an introduction to a 2,000-word essay
(b) Some repetition of phrases and ideas (e.g. modern/today)
(c) No sources given for ideas (e.g. the inseparable relationship . . .)
(d) No specific mention of the motivation theories to be discussed
(e) No mention of which Japanese car producer will be focused on

3 *Practice exercise: Rewriting*

Issues:

> No mention of Japanese company
> Short sentences – more links needed to organise the discussion
> Some repetition

> It has been shown that the hierarchy of needs theory of Maslow, Herzberg's two-factor theory and the achievement theory of McClelland have some relevance to the motivation of British employees, and the application of these theories has sometimes resulted in increased employee performance. However, some limitations to the application of these theories have been demonstrated, using the experience of the Toyota Company in its British factories. Cross-cultural problems have arisen with regard to Japanese expectations and British attitudes to work. Furthermore, it appears that knowledge workers need different motivation methods, since the older theories of motivation are not always relevant to today's workplace, where a more up-to-date theoretical basis is needed.

4 Proof-reading

(b) (i)   Africa is not a country: *such as Nigeria*

    (ii)   innocence is a noun: *Young and innocent*

    (iii) commas needed: *some manufacturers, for instance Toyota,*

    (iv) all verbs need to use past tense: *that produced*

    (v)   'successfulness' is not a word: *success*

    (vi) 'pervious' is incorrect: *previous*

    (vii) 'concept' is singular: *plays*

    (viii) repetition: *the essay will conclude with an analysis of*

    (ix) time periods need definite article: *the nineteenth century*

    (x)   *when consumers go out shopping*

(c) (i)   style – use children

    (i)   singular/plural – their lines

    (iii) vocabulary –torment is too strong, use inconvenience

    (iv) word ending – different effects

    (v)   factual – 1973

    (vi) word order – overcome

    (vii) punctuation – no comma needed

    (viii) spelling – Hungary

    (ix) missing word – the world

    (x)   tense: have entered

(d) Model answer:

Many non-European businesses are aiming to enter <u>the</u> single European market as they see an unexploited potential there. There are <u>two</u> reasons <u>for</u> this interest. Firstly, the non-European organisations are keen <u>to do business</u> in the European <u>market</u> because it is one of <u>the</u> leading investment <u>destinations</u> and <u>the</u> easiest place to set up and run a business. Secondly, the single European market <u>provides</u> <u>foreign</u> investors with an internationally competitive tax environment.

5 Confusing pairs

(a) principles

(b) lose

(c) affect

(d) compliments

(e) its

(f) economic

(g) accepted

ANSWERS: PART 2

2.1 Argument and discussion

3 *Practice exercise: Argument and discussion*

+	–
saves commuting time	employees may feel isolated
gives employees more flexibility	may not suit all employees
saves expensive office space	home may contain distractions
	requires different management style

Outline with structure (a)

(a) Introduction: reasons for growth home-working: development in communication technology, demand for more flexible work patterns.
(b) Drawbacks: Employees may feel isolated, be distracted by activities at home.
    May not suit all employees, some prefer more direct management.
(c) Benefits: Companies need to provide less office space, less time spent on commuting = more work time, employees have more flexibility.
(d) Discussion: Of benefit to certain employees in some roles, but necessary to have regular contact with colleagues and managers.

5 *Counter-arguments*

Sample answers:

It has been claimed that employees may waste time at home, but in practice there seems little evidence for this.

Although home-working may save companies money by reducing the need for office space, employees need to have a well-equipped workspace in their home.

6 *Providing evidence*

1   Drawbacks of imports – Inglehart
2   Benefits of imports – Indian case study (Goldberg *et al.*)
3   Writer's viewpoint

7 *Practice exercise: Argument and discussion*

Model answer:

It is widely thought that inflation is undesirable. Patterson (1998) points out that it can lead to industrial disputes as employees frequently demand pay rises to compensate for its effects, while excessive inflation results in lack of trust in money and uncertainty about the future. In contrast, Costa *et al.* (2000) demonstrate the advantages of moderate inflation in terms of stimulating spending and effectively reducing the value of debt. Clearly the issue must be the level of inflation, and in practice most governments seem to encourage inflation levels of about 2 per cent.

2.2 Cause and effect

2 Practice exercise: Cause and effect

Possible answers:

(a) Owing to the cold winter of 1995 there was an increased demand for electricity.
(b) Tax cuts often lead to higher levels of spending.
(c) Because of the introduction of digital cameras there was reduced demand for photographic film.
(d) As a result of interest rates being increased last spring there have been higher levels of saving.
(e) Falling sales of a firm's products can result in redundancies.
(f) His aggressive managerial style caused an increase in labour disputes.

3 Practice exercise: Cause and effect

Model answers:

(a) Increasing use of the internet for shopping has increased the number of delivery services.
(b) Rising demand for MBA courses led to tighter selection criteria being used.
(c) Lower fuel prices resulted in higher profits for freight companies.
(d) Bad weather in the Brazilian coffee-producing region caused a significant rise in coffee prices.
(e) The company's bankruptcy was due to careless accounting.
(f) The drop in share prices was caused by a steep rise in unemployment.
(g) Hiring extra staff resulted from winning a new contract.
(h) A significant rise in profits was owing to the sharp depreciation of the dollar.

4 Practice exercise: Cause and effect

(a) due to/owing to/produced by/because of/as a result of
(b) caused by/produced by/created by
(c) due to/because of/resulting from/caused by
(d) owing to/due to/because of
(e) lead to/cause/produce/result in/create
(f) results in/produces/causes/leads to
(g) results in/produces/causes/leads to

5 Practice exercise: Cause and effect

Model paragraph:

> An increase of 25 per cent in the price of oil would have numerous results. Firstly, it would lead to sharp rises in the cost of transport and freight, thus affecting the price of most goods. Clearly, businesses for which fuel was a significant proportion of their costs, such as airlines, would find it difficult to maintain profitability. Another consequence would be a reduction in oil consumption as marginal users switched to alternative fuels, such as gas, or made economies. There would also be increased investment in exploration for oil, as the oil companies attempted to increase supply, and this in turn would stimulate demand for equipment such as oil rigs. Finally, there would be a number of more localised effects, for instance a change in demand from larger to smaller and more economical vehicles.

2.3 Cohesion

2 Practice exercise: Cohesion

Reference	Reference word/phrase
La Ferrera	She
new businesses	they
average life of only 4.7 years	this
one economic	the former
one social	the latter
the former . . . the latter . . .	these

4 Practice exercise: Cohesion

(a) It   (b) he   (c) them (d) This (e) his   (f) they   (g) he

5 Practice exercise: Cohesion

Velcro is a fabric fastener used with clothes and shoes. **It** was invented by a Swiss engineer called George de Mestral. **His** idea was derived from studying the tiny hooks found on some plant seeds. **They** cling to animals and help disperse the seeds. **He** spent eight years perfecting **his** invention, which **he** called 'Velcro' from the French words 'velour' and 'crochet'. **It** was patented in 1955 and today over 60 million metres of **it** are sold annually.

6 Practice exercise: Cohesion

Model answer:

Wallace Carothers, the director of research at the American DuPont Corporation, invented nylon in 1935. He had previously studied chemistry, and specialised in polymers. They are molecules composed of long chains of atoms. Nylon was a strong but fine synthetic fibre which was first mass produced in 1939. It was used to make a wide range of products. These included stockings, toothbrushes, parachutes, fishing lines and surgical thread.

2.4 Comparisons

2 Practice exercise: Comparisons

(a) Residential property in London is twice as expensive as in Rome.
(b) Property in Moscow is slightly cheaper than in New York.
(c) Tokyo property is nearly as expensive as property in Paris.
(d) Singapore has significantly cheaper property than New York.
(e) London is the most expensive of the eight cities, while Sydney is the cheapest.

Possible answers:

(f) Parisian property is slightly cheaper than Moscow property.
(g) Property in Sydney is 50 per cent cheaper than in New York.

5 *Practice exercise: Comparisons*

(a) Real Madrid was the richest club **in world football.**
(b) Real Madrid's income was twice **as** much as AS Roma's.
(c) FC Barcelona earned **slightly** less than Manchester United.
(d) Chelsea had a significantly **higher** income than Liverpool.
(e) Internazionale had less revenue **than** AC Milan.

6 *Practice exercise: Comparisons*

(a) variations
(b) four
(c) as
(d) slightly
(e) than
(f) twice

7 *Practice exercise: Comparisons*

Sample paragraph:

The table shows the ten countries with the highest per-capita GDP, adjusted for PPP. The richest, Luxembourg, has a figure twice as high as Austria or Sweden. Norway, the second richest country in terms of spending power, is significantly richer than Singapore and the USA. Ireland, Switzerland and the Netherlands all have similar figures, while Austria is slightly better off than Sweden and Iceland.

8 *Practice exercise: Comparisons*

Sample paragraph:

The table compares two large UK supermarket chains, Sainsbury's and Morrisons. Sainsbury's is significantly larger than Morrisons, with 50 per cent higher turnover and nearly twice as many stores. Sainsbury's pre-tax profits are also 50 per cent higher, but their operating margins are significantly lower. Finally, Sainsbury's share of the market, at 16 per cent, is only a third larger than Morrisons'.

2.5 Definitions

1 *Simple definitions*

Model answers:

(a) loan
(b) organisation
(c) period
(d) agreement
(e) costs/expenses
(f) investor
(g) financial instrument

(h) A trades union is an organisation of workers formed to protect its members' interests.

(i) A monopoly is a market in which one company has total or near-total control.

(j) Marketing is a process that focuses on identifying and satisfying consumer demand profitably.

(k) A dividend is a payment made by a company to its shareholders.

(l) A hostile takeover is the acquisition of a firm despite the opposition of its management board.

2 *Complex definitions*

(a) a failed project

(b) development

(c) electronic commerce

(d) corporate governance

(e) globalisation

(f) empathy

(i) a   (ii) c   (iii) f   (iv) b, d   (v) e

3 *Practice exercise: Definitions*

Model answers:

(a) **Managing diversity** policies are a systematic and comprehensive managerial process for developing an environment in which all employees, with their similarities and differences, can contribute to the organisation, and where no-one is excluded due to unrelated factors.

(b) An **entrepreneurial business** is set up by somebody who demonstrates effective application of a number of enterprising attributes, such as creativity, initiative, risk taking, problem solving ability and autonomy, and will often risk his or her own capital.

(c) **Organisational culture** is a pattern of shared assumptions that the group learned as it solved its problems, which has proved itself and so is considered valid, and is passed on to new members.

(d) **Perfect competition** is characterised by a market so open that no participant can influence prices, without barriers to entry and with large numbers of buyers and sellers.

2.6 Examples

1 *Using examples*

(a) illustration

(b) support

(c) illustration

2 *Phrases to introduce examples*

Model answers:

(a) Some twentieth-century inventions, such as TV and the internet, affected the lives of most people.

(b) A number of sports, for example motor racing, have become very profitable due to the sale of television rights.

(c) Various companies have built their reputation on the strength of one product, a case in point is Microsoft Windows.
(d) Some brands, for instance confectionery such as Mars bars, have remained successful for more than 50 years.
(e) In recent years the product life cycle has tended to become shorter, particularly with electronic goods.
(f) A variety of products, e.g. shampoos, are promoted by celebrity endorsement.
(g) Speculation in some commodities, such as oil, has created price bubbles.
(h) Investors are often advised to spread their risk by putting their money into a range of investments, for instance equities, bonds and commodities.

3 Practice exercise: Examples

Possible answers:

Customs: holidays and festivals, ways of greeting people
Everyday patterns: types of shop, shop opening times
Inevitable differences: language, currency
Rapid changes of mood: depression, elation
Relatively short period: two/three months
Some aspects of their new surroundings: freedom, independence

4 Restatement

(a) The company's overheads, in other words the fixed costs, doubled last year.
(b) During a bear market, that is a period of falling share prices, few investors make money.
(c) The Indian capital, namely New Delhi, has a thriving commercial centre.
(d) The last day of the 2008–9 financial year, i.e. 31 March, was a Tuesday.

2.7 Generalisations

2 Structure

(b) Job satisfaction is not always related to the rate of pay.
(c) A weak currency tends to raise a country's level of exports.
(d) Spending on R & D is often linked to the introduction of new products.
(e) High rates of unemployment normally reduce the level of consumer spending.
(f) Cold weather is likely to increase demand for gas.

3 Over-generalising

(a) Accurate
(b) Unemployment in 2009 was higher than in 1999 or 1989.
(c) Interest rates were lower in 2009 than in 1999 or 1989.
(d) Accurate
(e) Inflation in 2009 was lower than in 1999 or 1989.

4 *Practice exercise: Generalisations*

Model sentences:

(a) Most attempts to replicate Silicon Valley in other countries have failed.
(b) The reasons for Silicon Valley's success have not been understood.
(c) There are three ways in which such centres can grow.
(d) A recession can lead to the growth of new companies.
(e) A business-friendly culture is vital for success.

2.8 Numbers

2 *Percentages*

(a) 50%   (b) 100%   (c) 400%

3 *Simplification*

(b) Scores of students applied for the scholarship.
(c) He rewrote the essay several/a few times.
(d) Dozens of books were published on the economic crisis.
(e) Various names were suggested but rejected for the new chocolate bar.

4 *Practice exercise: Numbers*

Model answers:

(a) The price of petrol has increased tenfold since 1975.
(b) Two thirds of the students in the group were women.
(c) The new high-speed train halved the journey time to Madrid.
(d) The number of students applying for the Management course has risen by 50 per cent.
(e) The number of visitors to the theme park doubled every year from 2007 to 2009.
(f) More than twice as many British students as Italian students complete their first degree course.
(g) Tap water is seven hundred times cheaper than bottled water.
(h) The highest rate of unemployment is in Spain and the lowest in Norway.
(i) A quarter of the garments produced had some kind of fault.
(j) A majority of shareholders supported the proposal, but a large proportion of these expressed some doubts.

5 *Practice exercise: Numbers*

Model answers:

(a) More than half the group were Chinese speakers.
(b) Management was the most popular future course.
(c) One fifth of the group planned to study Economics.
(d) Only one student was over 23.
(e) Swimming was the favourite sport of one third of the group.
(f) The least popular sports were cycling and tennis.

2.9 Problems and solutions

3 *Practice exercise: Problems and solutions*

Problem	Many developing countries have found that the development of a tourism industry can bring social and environmental drawbacks . . .
Solution A	One possible solution is to target upmarket holidaymakers, in order to get the maximum profit from minimum numbers.
Argument against solution A	However, this is a limited market and requires considerable investment in infrastructure and training.
Solution B	Another remedy is to rigorously control the environmental standards of any development, in order to minimise the impact of the construction.
Conclusion in favour of B	This requires effective government agencies, but is likely to ensure the best outcome for both tourists and locals.

5 *Practice exercise: Problems and solutions*

Model argument:

> Currently there is increasing demand for university places, which frequently leads to overcrowding of student facilities. It has been argued that fees should be increased to reduce demand for places, but this would discriminate against students from poorer families. Another proposal is for the government to pay for the expansion of universities, but against this is the view that this would unfairly benefit the minority who in any case go on to earn higher salaries. A fairer solution might be for the government to subsidise the fees of the poorest students.

2.10 Style

3 *Practice exercise: Style*

Model sentences:

(a) The main factor in the collapse of Enron was . . .
(b) There appears to be a significant risk of inflation increasing.
(c) It is commonly believed that the economy is deteriorating.
(d) After 1989 the price of Japanese property fell sharply.
(e) The numbers in that report are unreliable.
(f) The Russian inflation led to poverty and social unrest.
(g) The manager was dismissed for embezzlement.
(h) Currently there is high unemployment.

4 Avoiding repetition and redundancy

Currently, fast food is growing in popularity. It is food that people can buy or cook quickly. This essay examines the advantages and drawbacks of fast food. First, it is usually tasty. Most people who work in offices are very busy, so they do not have time to go home for lunch. But they can eat in McDonalds' restaurants. The second benefit of fast food is cheapness. As it is produced in large quantities, this means that the companies can keep costs down. As a result it is usually less expensive than a meal in a conventional restaurant.

5 Varying sentence length

Model answer:

(a) Worldwide, enrolments in higher education are increasing. In developed countries over half of all young people enter college, while similar trends are seen in China and South America. This growth has put financial strain on state university systems, so that many countries are asking students and parents to contribute. This leads to a debate about whether students or society benefit from tertiary education.

(b) China is one developing country (but not the only one) which has imposed fees on students since 1997. The results have been surprising: enrolments, especially in the most expensive universities, have continued to rise steeply, growing 200 per cent overall between 1997 and 2001. It seems in this case that higher fees attract rather than discourage students, who see them as a sign of a good education. They compete more fiercely for places, leading to the result that a place at a good college can cost $5000 per year for fees and maintenance.

2.11 Visual information

1 The language of change

Types	Uses	Example
1 diagram	d	E
2 table	f	B
3 map	a	F
4 pie chart	c	D
5 bar chart	b	C
6 line graph	e	A

2 Practice exercise: Visual information

(a) rose/increased
(b) levelled off
(c) steadily
(d) peaked
(e) fell/decreased

3 Describing visuals

(a) (i) is better. It comments on the main features of the chart but does not repeat the statistics.

(b) Model answers:

  (a) density
  (b) demonstrates/illustrates
  (c) between
  (d) less-crowded/less densely populated
  (e) role/part
  (f) since/as/because
  (g) tend

5 Practice exercise: Visual information

Model answers:

(a) shows
(b) French
(c) figure
(d) countries/states
(e) than
(f) higher

6 Practice exercise: Visual information

Model paragraph:

The table shows the world's ten largest companies by revenue in 2008. It is noticeable that seven of the ten, including the two largest, Shell and Exxon, are oil companies. The third largest, Wal-Mart, is a multinational retailer, and the eighth, ING Group, is a bank. Three of the companies recorded a loss during this period, the largest, over $16 billion, by Conoco Phillips.

2.12 Working in groups

1 Group work

(a) F   (b) T   (c) F   (d) F   (e) T   (f) F

2 Making group work successful

1   Get to know the other members.
2   Make everyone feel included.
3   Analyse the task.
4   Plan the job and the responsibilities.
5   Divide up the work fairly, according to the abilities of the members.
6   Select a co-ordinator/editor.
7   Finish the assignment on time.

3 Dealing with problems

(a)(i)   The lazy students will learn nothing from this approach, and the same problem will occur next time they are involved in group work.

(a)(ii) Although it may seem difficult, this is the only positive solution.

(a)(iii) Your teachers are unlikely to help – group work is designed to make these problems your responsibility.

(b)(i)   Your teachers are unlikely to help – group work is designed to make these problems your responsibility.

(b)(ii) This will not help you in the long run – you must learn to take part in discussion.

(b)(iii) The right approach. The other members probably don't realise that you are having difficulties with their language.

(c)(i)   If everyone in the group takes part the offender will be forced to accept that their behaviour is unhelpful.

(c)(ii) Your teachers are unlikely to help – group work is designed to make these problems your responsibility.

(c)(iii) You will run the risk that they will get a poor mark and so everyone will suffer.

 # ANSWERS: PART 3

3.1 Abbreviations

6 Practice exercise: Abbreviations

(a) information and communications technology/and others
(b) unique selling point
(c) that is/the World Trade Organisation
(d) note/curricula vitae/Human Resources
(e) The Organisation for Economic and Cultural Development/the United Arab Emirates
(f) The European Union/Value Added Tax
(g) The Chief Executive Officer/Research and Development
(h) Figure 4/world wide web
(i) British Airways/Hong Kong/Kuala Lumpur
(j) Public relations/$75,000
(k) With reference to/Annual General Meeting/as soon as possible
(l) Professor/Master of Science/Doctor of Philosophy

3.2 Academic vocabulary

2 Practice exercise: Academic vocabulary

(a) predicted
(b) significant
(c) varied

(d) created
(e) hypothetical
(f) invested
(g) emphasis/reliability
(h) evaluated
(i) indicative or indicators
(j) contributory

3 Practice exercise: Academic vocabulary

(a) significant or contributory
(b) distributed
(c) achievements
(d) definitive
(e) analysed or evaluated
(f) indicators/predictors/variables

5 Practice exercise: Academic vocabulary

(a) irrelevant
(b) subjective or irrational
(c) concrete or relevant
(d) approximate or rough
(e) relative
(f) logical or rational
(g) theoretical or abstract

3.3 Articles

4 Practice exercise: Using 'the'

(a) Engineering is the main industry in **the** northern region.
(b) Insurance firms have made a record profit in **the** financial year 2008–9.
(c) Global warming is partly caused by fossil fuels.
(d) **The** company's CEO has been arrested on fraud charges.
(e) Theft is costing **the** banking business millions of pounds a year.
(f) Tourism is **the** world's biggest industry.
(g) **The** forests of Scandinavia produce most of Britain's paper.
(h) **The** Thai currency is **the** baht.
(i) Computer crime has grown by 200 per cent in **the** last decade.
(j) **The** main causes of **the** industrial revolution are still debated.
(k) Already 3 per cent of **the** working population are employed in call centres.
(l) **The** latest forecast predicts rising unemployment for two years.
(m) Research on **the** housing market is being conducted in **the** business school.
(n) **The** best definition is often **the** simplest.

5 Practice exercise: Articles

(a)   –
(b)   –
(c)   the
(d)   –
(e)   –
(f)   the
(g)   the
(h)   the
(i)   –
(j)   an
(k)   the
(l)   the
(m) the
(n)   –

3.4 Caution

2 Using modals, adverbs and verbs

(Others are possible)

Modals: might/may/could/should
Adverbs: often/usually/frequently/generally/commonly/mainly
Verb/phrase: seems to/appears to/in general/by and large/it appears/it seems

3 Practice exercise: Caution

Model answers:

(a) Private companies are often more efficient than state-owned businesses.
(b) In general workers prefer pay cuts to redundancy.
(c) Older students may perform better at university than younger ones.
(d) Word-of-mouth is commonly the best kind of advertising.
(e) English pronunciation can be confusing.
(f) Introducing new models of products tends to help to increase sales.
(g) Global warming might cause the sea level to rise.
(h) Most shopping may done on the internet in ten years' time.

4 Practice exercise: Caution

(a) The company's efforts to save energy were quite/fairly successful.
(b) The survey was (a fairly/quite a) comprehensive study of student opinion.
(c) His second book had a rather hostile reception.
(d) The first year students were quite fascinated by her lectures.
(e) The decision to invest the pension fund in commercial property was rather disastrous.

6 Practice exercise: Caution

Model answer:

> One way to confront the threat of global warming **may be** for governments to encourage 'green' industries with subsidies. By encouraging investment in wind or solar power, not only **could** carbon emissions be reduced, but more jobs **might** be created. **It is possible that** two problems **would** be solved at the same time; unemployment and CO_2 production. It is **estimated** that spending on environmental technology **may** grow by 5 per cent a year until 2020. By then **probably** hundreds of millions of people worldwide **might** be working in recycling and carbon-neutral energy projects, and the danger of global warming **would** be significantly reduced.

3.5 Linkers

1 Identifying linkers

(a) A few inventions, <u>for instance</u> television, have had a major impact on everyday life.
(b) <u>In addition</u>, a large volume of used cars are sold through dealerships.
(c) The definition of motivation is important <u>since</u> it is the cause of some disagreement.
(d) The technology allows consumers a choice, <u>thus</u> increasing their sense of satisfaction.
(e) Four hundred people were interviewed for the survey, <u>then</u> the results were analysed.
(f) <u>However</u>, another body of opinion associates globalisation with unfavourable outcomes.
     (ii) d
     (iii) c
     (iv) f
     (v) a
     (vi) e

2 Practice exercise: Using linkers

Linker	Type	Linker	Type
(a) such as	example	(f) in other words	example
(b) but	opposition	(g) instead of	opposition
(c) Although	opposition	(h) Consequently	result
(d) for instance	example	(i) and	addition
(e) however	opposition	(j) neither . . . nor	opposition

3 Practice exercise: Linkers

(Others are possible)

Addition: moreover/as well as/in addition/and/also/furthermore
Result: therefore/consequently/so/that is why (see Unit 2.2)
Reason: because/owing to/as a result of/as/since/due to (see Unit 2.2)
Time: after/while/then/next/subsequently (see Unit 3.12)
Example: such as/e.g./in particular/for instance (see Unit 2.6)
Opposition: but/yet/while/however/nevertheless/whereas/albeit/although/despite

4 Practice exercise: Linkers

Model answers:

(a) such as
(b) yet
(c) and (or: so that/consequently)
(d) Although
(e) for instance
(f) since
(g) for instance
(h) Moreover
(i) because
(j) However

5 Linkers of opposition

Model answers:

(a) (i) Although the government claimed that inflation was falling, the opposition said it was rising.
    (ii) The government claimed that inflation was falling while the opposition said it was rising.
(b) (i) This department must reduce expenditure, yet it needs to install new computers.
    (ii) While this department must reduce expenditure it also needs to install new computers.
(c) (i) In spite of being heavily advertised sales of the new car were poor.
    (ii) Sales of the new car were poor despite being heavily advertised.

3.6 Nouns and adjectives

2 Practice exercise: Nouns and adjectives

Noun	Adjective	Noun	Adjective
approximation	approximate	particularity	particular
superiority	superior	reason	reasonable
strategy	strategic	synthesis	synthetic
politics	political	economy	economic/al
industry	industrial	culture	cultural
exterior	external	average	average
height	high	reliability	reliable
heat	hot	strength	strong
confidence	confident	truth	true
width	wide	probability	probable
necessity	necessary	length	long
danger	dangerous	relevance	relevant

3 Practice exercise: Nouns and adjectives

(a) confident
(b) particularity/strength

(c) probability
(d) relevant
(e) necessary
(f) average
(g) danger
(h) necessity
(i) unreliable
(j) Confidence
(k) economic
(l) synthesis

4 Practice exercise: Nouns and adjectives

(a) strategic – strategy
(b) analytical – analysis
(c) synthetic – synthesis
(d) major – majority
(e) cultural – culture
(f) theoretical – theory
(g) frequent – frequency
(h) critical – criticism/critic
(i) Social – society
(j) practical – practice

5 Abstract nouns

(a) cause (of)
(b) theory
(c) event
(d) feature
(e) machine
(f) area
(g) (an) organisation
(h) views
(i) worry
(j) process
(k) types
(l) problem

3.7 Prefixes and suffixes

2 Prefixes

auto	by itself
co	together
ex	previous
ex	outside

macro   large
micro   small
multi   many
over   too much
post   later
re   again
sub   below
under   below
under   not enough

3 Practice exercise: Prefixes and suffixes

(a) social class at bottom of society
(b) more tickets sold than seats available
(c) very local climate
(d) economy based on information not production
(e) not listed in the telephone book
(f) disappointed

7 Practice exercise: Prefixes and suffixes

(a) noun – withdrawal of a service
(b) adjective – two related events at the same time
(c) adverb – without cooperation
(d) adjective – related to evolution
(e) noun – person who protests
(f) adjective – not able to be forecast
(g) adjective – able to be sold
(h) noun – person being interviewed
(i) noun – belief that increasing consumption benefits society
(j) adverb – in a way that suggests a symbol

8 Practice exercise: Prefixes and suffixes

(a) joint production/junior company
(b) without choosing to/not hurt
(c) able to be refilled/certain
(d) cannot be provided/unusual
(e) existing in theory/breaking into pieces

3.8 Prepositions

1 The main uses of prepositions

purpose of/development of/in Catalonia/over the period/contributed to/valuable for/In conclusion/sets out/relationship between/decline in/supply of/in the factory context

Verb + = contributed to
Adj + = valuable for
Phrasal verb = sets out
Place = in Catalonia/in the factory context
Time = over the period
Phrase = In conclusion

2 *Practice exercise: Prepositions*

(b) adjective +
(c) verb +
(d) preposition of place
(e) noun +
(f) phrase
(g) preposition of place
(h) preposition of time

3 *Practice exercise: Prepositions and nouns*

(a) of (b) in (c) of (d) to (e) in (f) on

4 *Practice exercise: Prepositions in phrases*

(a) on (b) of (c) of (d) in (e) of (f) on (g) in (h) of

5 *Practice exercise: Prepositions of place and time*

(a) Among
(b) from, to/between, and
(c) in, of
(d) in, in
(e) in, at
(f) On, between

6 *Practice exercise: Prepositions*

(a) out	(b) of	(c) in/to	(d) to	(e) among/in	(f) from/in
(g) between	(h) in	(i) of	(j) in/over	(k) between	(l) in
(m) in	(n) of	(o) to/in			

3.9 Punctuation

7 *Practice exercise: Punctuation*

(a) The study was carried out by Christine Zhen-Wei Qiang of the World Bank.
(b) Professor Rowan's new book 'The Triumph of Capitalism' is published in New York.
　 or
　 Professor Rowan's new book *The Triumph of Capitalism* is published in New York.

(c) As Keynes said: 'It's better to be roughly right than precisely wrong'.
(d) Three departments, Law, Business and Economics, have had their funding cut.
(e) As Cammack (1994) points out: 'Latin America is creating a new phenomenon; democracy without citizens.'
(f) Thousands of new words such as 'app' enter the English language each year.
(g) In 2005 France's per-capita GDP was 73 per cent of America's.
(h) She scored 56 per cent on the main course; the previous semester she had achieved 67 per cent.

8 Practice exercise: Punctuation

The London School of Business is offering three new courses this year: Economics with Psychology, Introduction to Management and e-commerce. The first is taught by Dr Jennifer Hillary and runs from October to January. The second, Introduction to Management, for MSc. Finance students is offered in the second semester, and is assessed by coursework only. Professor Wang's course in e-commerce runs in both the autumn and the spring, and is for more experienced students.

3.10 Singular or plural?

1 Five problem areas

(a) . . . and disadvantages	(e)	
(b) are vaccinated	(a)	
(c) rural areas	(c)	
(d) . . . in crime	(b)	
(e) Each company has its own policy	(d)	

4 Practice exercise: Singular or plural?

(a) Little
(b) businesses
(c) experience/is
(d) travel broadens
(e) Paper was
(f) much advice
(g) few interests
(h) civil war
(i) Irons were
(j) work

5 Practice exercise: Singular or plural?

companies have/websites/e-commerce/this is/businesses/their/trouble/security/expense/ mean/these companies

3.11 Synonyms

1 Using synonyms

word/phrase	synonym
largest	giant
oil	hydrocarbon
company	firm
in the world	global/internationally
people	employees

3 Practice exercise: Synonyms

(Others are possible)

(a) Professor Hicks <u>challenged</u> the <u>results</u> of the <u>study</u>.
(b) The <u>figures</u> <u>demonstrate</u> a steady <u>increase</u> in applications.
(c) The institute's <u>forecast</u> has caused a major <u>debate</u>.
(d) Cost seems to be the <u>principal disadvantage</u> to that <u>method</u>.
(e) They will <u>focus on</u> the first <u>possibility</u>.
(f) After the lecture she tried to <u>explain</u> her <u>theory</u>.
(g) Three <u>topics</u> need to be <u>evaluated</u>.
(h) The <u>structure</u> can be <u>kept</u> but the <u>aim</u> needs to be <u>modified</u>.
(i) OPEC, the oil producers' cartel, is to <u>reduce output</u> to <u>increase</u> global prices.
(j) The <u>tendency</u> to smaller families has <u>accelerated</u> in the last decade.

4 Practice exercise: Synonyms

UK – British – this country
agency – organisation – body
advertising campaign – publicity programme – advertising blitz
to raise – to improve
British eating habits – regular hand washing
to cut – reduction

5 Practice exercise: Synonyms

firm's plan
cut expenditure or spending
business intends or proposes
earnings or salaries
employees
raised

3.12 Time words

3 Practice exercise: Time words

(a) Last
(b) During/On

(c) By
(d) for
(e) ago
(f) later
(g) until
(h) Currently/Now

4 Practice exercise: Time words

(a) Recently
(b) until
(c) for
(d) Last month
(e) by
(f) Since
(g) During

5 Practice exercise: Time words

(a) In/Over
(b) Since
(c) ago
(d) recently
(e) Currently
(f) by
(g) since

6 Practice exercise: Time words

(a) until
(b) later
(c) after/in
(d) During
(e) By/In
(f) for
(g) since
(h) after
(i) until
(j) before

3.13 Verbs – passives

1 Active and passive

(a) The data was collected and the two groups (were) compared.
(b) 120 people in three social classes were interviewed.
(c) The results were checked and several errors (were) found.

(d) An analysis of the findings will be made.
(e) Four managers were asked to give their opinions.

2 Using adverbs

(Other adverb combinations possible)

(a) The company was profitably run by the Connors family until 1981.
(b) The reasons for the Asian currency crisis were vigorously debated (by economists).
(c) All students in the exam were helpfully provided with pencils.
(d) A presentation was vividly given by the staff of the advertising agency.
(e) The percentages were accurately calculated to three decimal places (by researchers).
(f) Their business was optimistically called the Grand Universal Trading Company.
(g) The life cycles of over 240 companies were carefully researched.

4 Practice exercise: Passives

Passive	Active possible?	Active
He was worn out	Yes	The effort . . . had worn him out
He was born	No	
John was concerned by	Yes	The situation of the poor concerned John . . .
a (. . .) shop which was called	Yes	which he called
the business was taken over	Yes	his wife took the business over
she was soon assisted	Yes	their 10-year-old son assisted her

The effect of using the passive throughout would be to make the tone very formal.

5 Practice exercise: Passives

Model text:

> In 1889 he was introduced to Florence Rowe, the daughter of a bookseller, while on holiday. After they were married her ideas affected the business: the product range was enlarged to include stationery and books. The Boots subscription library and in-store cafes were also introduced due to Florence's influence. During the First World War the Boots factories made a variety of products, from sterilizers to gas masks. But after the war Jesse was attacked by arthritis and, worried by the economic prospects, he sold the company to an American rival for £2m. This, however, went bankrupt during the Depression and Boots was then bought by a British group for £6m, and Jesse's son, John became chairman. The famous No.7 cosmetics range was launched in the 1930s and in the Second World War the factories produced both saccharin and penicillin. However, recently the company has been threatened by intense competition from supermarkets in its core pharmaceutical business.

3.14 Verbs of reference

3 Practice exercise: Verbs of reference

(a) A admitted that he might have made a mistake. . . .
(b) B denied saying that women make better managers than men.
(c) C stated/claimed/argued that small firms are more dynamic than large ones.
(d) D agreed with C's views on small firms.
(e) E assumed that most people work for money.
(f) F concluded that bonds are the best long-term investment.
(g) G doubted that electric cars would replace conventional ones.
(h) H suggested that the reasons for employee turnover in call centres should be investigated.
(i) I hypothesised a link between the business cycle and sunspot activity.

5 Practice exercise: Verbs of reference

(a) L criticised her research methods.
(b) M identified/classified four main types of business start-up.
(c) N commended the company for its pattern of corporate governance.
(d) O interpreted the results as showing over-reliance on a shrinking market.
(e) P identified three airlines as likely to make a profit this year.
(f) Q described Keynes as the most influential economist of the twentieth century.
(g) R defined a bond as a financial instrument giving a fixed return over a limited period.
(h) S characterised/portrayed entrepreneurs as hard-working, imaginative risk-takers.

3.15 Verbs – tenses

1 Tenses in academic writing

	Tense	Reason for use
a	Present simple	General rule
b	present continuous	current situation
c	present perfect	recent unfinished event
d	present perfect continuous	recent, with emphasis on action that continues for a long time
e	simple past	finished, with time phrase
f	past continuous	finished, with emphasis on action that continues for a long time
g	past perfect	refers to a previous past period
h	'will' future	prediction

2 Practice exercise: Tenses

(a) has risen/has been rising
(b) stands for
(c) sold
(d) had taken out

(e) will have
(f) is considering
(g) was building/had built
(h) disputed
(i) has fallen/has been falling

4 *Practice exercise: Tenses*

(a) is working
(b) believes
(c) is looking for
(d) is running
(e) rose
(f) owns
(g) live
(h) is attending

6 *Practice exercise: Tenses*

(a) met
(b) was
(c) agreed
(d) allows (generally, at any time)
(e) support
(f) face
(g) have
(h) spends
(i) will give
(j) will make
(k) will be

ANSWERS: PART 4

4.1 Formal letters and emails

1 *Letters*

(a) address of sender
(b) address of recipient
(c) sender's reference
(d   date
(e) greeting
(f) subject headline
(g) reason for writing

(h) further details
(i) request for response
(j) ending
(k) signature
(l) writer's name and job title

2 Practice exercise: Formal letters

See below for model answer.

4 Practice exercise: Emails

Sender = student/recipient = teacher

Reply is unlikely, unless recipient needs to comment on the attached paper.

---

54 Sydney Road
Rowborough RB1 6FD

Mr M. Bramble
Administrative Assistant
Central Admissions Office
Wye House
Park Campus
University of Mercia
Borchester BR3 5HT

5th May 2010

Dear Mr Bramble,

Informal Interview: Yr Ref: MB/373

Thank you for inviting me to interview on 21 May. I will be able to attend on that date, but it would be much more convenient if I could have the interview at 12, due to the train times from Rowborough.

Could you please let me know if this alteration is possible?

Yours sincerely,

P. Tan

P. Tan

5 *Practice exercise: Emails*

Model answers:

(a) Hi Mark,
    We need to schedule a short meeting tomorrow. What time would suit you?
    See you soon,
(b) Hello Tricia,
    I'm looking for another source for this month's essay. Could you recommend something suitable?
    Best wishes,
(c) Hi everyone,
    It's only a week before the end of the course – what are we going to do to celebrate? Let me have your ideas – I'll pass them on and hopefully get something good fixed up for Sat 12th!
(d) Dear Tim Carey,
    I've never had this book, so I can't return it. Can you check your records please?

4.3 Designing and reporting surveys

1 *Conducting surveys*

(Other suggestions possible/in any order)

Get up-to-date data
Collect information about the behaviour of a specific group, e.g. clients of a firm
Check/replicate other research

2 *Questionnaire design*

(a) (ii) is less embarrassing for most people to answer.
(b) (i) is an open question and has many possible answers.
    (ii) is a closed question with a limited range of responses.
(c) For casual interviews ten is probably the maximum most interviewees will cope with.

3 *Practice exercise: Reporting surveys*

(a)   conducted
(b)   random
(c)   questionnaire
(d)   questioned
(e)   respondents/interviewees
(f)   Interviewees/Respondents
(g)   mentioned
(h)   majority
(i)   slightly
(j)   minority
(k)   questions

(l)   common
(m)   generally
(n)   sample

4 Practice exercise: Designing and reporting surveys

Model questions: (3–6 could use present tense)

Q2 Why did you take a job?
Q3 What effect did the work have on your studies?
Q4 What kind of work did you do?
Q5 What hours did you work?
Q6 How much did you earn?
Q7 Do you have any comments on your work?

5 Practice exercise: Designing and reporting surveys

(a)   past tense
(b)   present tense (the survey is completed but the results are still valid)

4.4 Taking ideas from sources

1 Can money buy happiness?

Model answer:

(e) (i)   Happiness often depends on feeling wealthier than others.
(e) (ii) People believe that leisure = happiness, so working longer to get extra goods won't lead
          to happiness.
(f)   Model answer:

          Another explanation Penec presents is that happiness is often dependent on a comparison
          with others, so that if neighbours are also getting richer there is no apparent improvement.
          A further factor relates to leisure, which is widely equated with happiness. Consequently
          the idea of increasing workload to be able to purchase more goods or services is not
          going to result in greater happiness.

Model answer:

(g)   Penec, A. (2003) 'The measurement of happiness', *Applied Econometrics* 44 pp. 18–27.

4.5 Writing longer essays

2 Practice exercise: Writing longer essays

(Model answers, others may be possible)

(a)   staff/workers/workforce
(b)   In most contemporary businesses the skills and performance of employees is an essential
      factor in the success of the enterprise.
(c)   Motivation, which has been defined as 'the direction or persistence of action', and describing
      'why do people do what they do' (Mullins 2006: 184).

(d) This essay will examine some of the main theories in this field, dividing them into the content theories such as Maslow's and the process theories characterised by Vroom's. An attempt will then be made to assess their relevance to the modern workplace, taking as an example the employment policies of Toyota in the UK.

(e) 'goal specificity, goal difficulty and goal commitment each served to enhance task performance' (Steers 2004: 382).

(f) Maslow's hierarchy of needs theory was first published in 1943 . . .

(g) He claimed that so-called hygiene factors such as conditions and pay were likely to cause negative attitudes if inadequate . . .

(h) It should be emphasised that these various approaches are by no means mutually exclusive. . . . In this respect the process theories accommodate better to the variations between different employees.

(i) In many ways Toyota's approach seems to conform closely to the Maslow/Herzberg model.

Index